HARDPRESS.NET
HOME OF HARD-TO-FIND BOOKS

The Amethyst
by Nathan Covington Brooks

Address:
HardPress
8345 NW 66TH ST #2561
MIAMI FL 33166-2626
USA
Email: info@hardpress.net

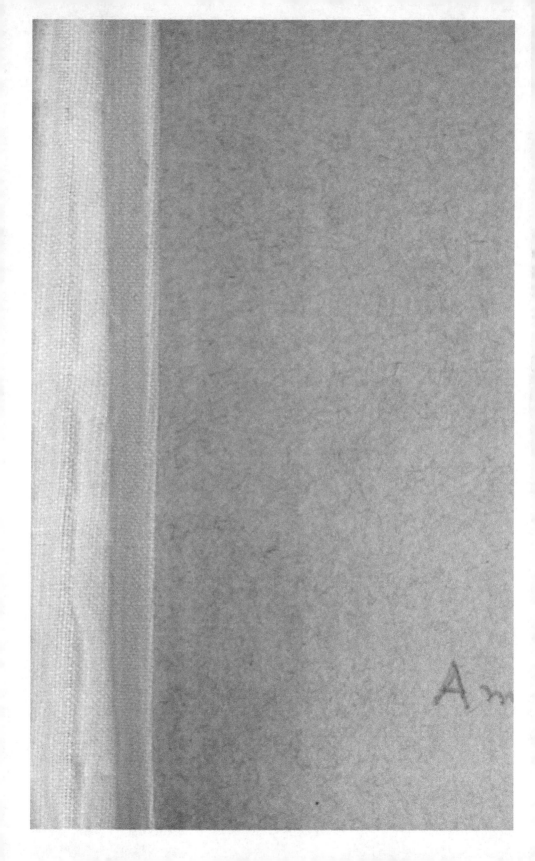

A𝓃

Mary G. Clifton

Æt. 4

for

J. 1824

STUDY.

Lith of Endicott & Swett.

THE
AMETHYST.

BALTIMORE,
PUB. BY N. C. BROOKS.
1831.

THE AMETHYST,

AN

ANUAL OF LITERATURE

EDITED AND PUBLISHED BY N. C. BROOKS.

DEAR TO THE HEART OF FRIENDSHIP BE
MY SIMPLE OFFERING, DESIGNED
TO WILE A WEARY HOUR, AND FREE
FROM GRIEVOUS CARES THE ANXIOUS MIND.

Baltimore:

PRINTED BY WILLIAM A. FRANCIS.

MDCCCXXXI.

DISTRICT OF MARYLAND, TO WIT:

BE IT REMEMBERED, That on the twenty-fifth day of September, in the fifty-fourth year of the Independence of the United States of America, Nathan C. Brooks, of the said district, has deposited in this office, the title of a book, the right whereof he claims as proprietor, in the words following, to wit:

'THE AMETHYST, an Annual of Literature. Edited and published by Nathan C. Brooks

Dear to the heart of Friendship be
My simple offering, designed
To wile a weary hour, and free
From grievous cares the anxious mind.'

In conformity to the Act of the Congress of the United States, entitled "An Act for the encouragement of learning, by securing the copies of maps, charts, and books, to the authors and proprietors of such copies, during the times therein mentioned;" and also to the act, entitled "An Act supplementary to the act, entitled "An Act for the encouragement of learning, by securing the copies of maps, charts, and books, to the authors and proprietors of such copies during the times therein mentioned;" and extending the benefits thereof to the arts of designing, engraving, etching historical and other prints."

PHILIP MOORE,
Clerk of the District of Maryland.

TO THE

REVEREND JAMES MAGRAW, D. D.

THIS VOLUME

IS MOST RESPECTFULLY INSCRIBED.

PREFACE.

In presenting the first number of the AMETHYST to the public, the Editor indulges the hope, that, if it should be found to be inferior to the other Annuals, the very late period of the year at which it was commenced, and the disadvantages under which a first publication of any Periodical labors, will be a sufficient apology for any seeming deficiencies.

Three months only have elapsed, since it was first contemplated to get up the Amethyst, a period so exceedingly short, that the Editor flatters himself no similar work of equal merit has ever been gotten up in the same time, in this country.

The literary articles, which are submitted to the public, are all original—the productions of writers of our own city, in the selection of which he has been careful to admit only such as might be, at once, interesting, innocent, and subservient to morality.

The Embellishments are Lithographic and were all designed expressly for the work. Their softness, beauty and delicate finish must, he thinks, render them pleasing to all.

It is purposed to continue the publication of the Amethyst in future, though in an enlarged form, with such literary improvements as may be derived from a more extensive correspondence.

To those writers who have generously exerted their talents in favor of the Amethyst, the Editor returns his most grateful acknowledgements as well as to M. Swett to whose talents he is indebted for the embellishments.

The Editor will thankfully receive from writers of talent throughout the country, for the next volume any contributions that may be forwarded by May 1st, 1831.

NATHAN C. BROOKS.

Baltimore, October 1st, 1830.

CONTENTS.

A*

CONTENTS.

EMBELLISHMENTS.

THE AMETHYST.

THE AMETHYST.

REFERRING TO THE VIGNETTE TITLE-PAGE.

THE Muses borne on airy wing,
   Have rang'd the fields of Poesy,
From bright and cultur'd flowers to bring
   A wreath of rarest, richest dye,

To deck, in amaranthine bloom,
   A classic treasure for the fair;
And shed a grateful, sweet perfume
   O'er all the sparkling beauties there.

They've brought rich gems of brilliance bright
   From mines of Fairyland, to throw
Their rays of coruscating light
   Upon its virgin page of snow.

They've breath'd o'er its enchanted leaves
  The sounds of fairy lute and lyre,
To soothe the care-worn heart that grieves
  And tranquil, joyous thoughts inspire.

Then will the kind and gentle fair
  The anxious Muses' task approve?
And take the simple offering dear
  To fancy, friendship and to love.

FRONTISPIECE

STUDY.

BY W. G. MOYSTON.

Lone in his midnight cell, remote from sound
Of the unheeding crowd, the student pores
O'er many an ancient tale of classic ground,
Or borne on fancy's pinions seeks the shores
Of Ilium, and where Scamander roars,
Revives each scene of memorable fight;
The Greeks' black ships or Troy's beleagur'd
      tow'rs,
Nor yet assents to close his aching sight
Till mark'd the morning star, the harbinger of
      light.

Perhaps some page he scans of native strain
Where science hath her treasury combin'd,
Or with some questionable story, vain
Regales the feverish palate of his mind;
In literary cloister close confin'd

He knows no joy beyond his dusky wall,
Pallid and meagre like a "ghost forpin'd,"
Who only wakes and walks at evening's fall,
And seeks his silent couch at rosy morning's call.

Such well may man; but yet not she, o'er whom
Sorrow and musing, which comes next, to pale
The lustre of the eye, and steal the bloom
Of health from off young cheeks, should ne'er pre
    vail;
Yet may she seek some sweet domestic tale
Or magic song in favorite tender tome,
Which turns the willing heart to mirth or wail,
Or tempers childhood's ardent wish to roam
And tells that purest joy is ever found at home.

Divine by birth! yet ah! diviner she
Who to corporeal grace and loveliness,
Adjoins a mind of spotless purity
Cultur'd by thought and stor'd against distress;
Well may she hope for lasting happiness;
Enlink'd for life with some congenial mind,
And with her consort win that promis'd bliss
Which wedded love hath yet in store design'd,
For those of gentle hearts and sentiments refin'd.

A NOCTURNAL REVERIE.

BY JOHN COLEMAN.

———

"We'll innocently steal celestial fire,
And kindle our devotion at the stars."

YOUNG.

———

I LOVE at the close of day to look out from my casement on the mild and tranquil beauty of our summer evening sky.—It is peculiarly agreeable to awake at such a time, and enjoy the cool and invigorating breezes which usually spring up and render these by far the most delightful hours of the twenty-four.—The spirit seems to recover from the lassitude and weariness which weighed it down during the sultry heat of the day; the body feels no longer that oppressive languor which a little while before ran through its sluggish veins: a soft and sweet feeling pervades the mind, and it insensibly sinks into the arms of pleasing con-

templation. Every thing around us, too, is calculated to assist the innocent delusions into which
we may be led by fancy's wild excursions. Sleep
wields

"Her leaden sceptre o'er a slumbering world;"

unbroken silence reigns profound; creation seems
hushed in the deep repose of the grave; and one
might easily conceive himself alone in the universe,—a solitary being in the vast temple of Nature's God!

I was thus sitting a few evenings ago. It was
a lovely night, just such an one as poets love to
praise, and painters strive in vain to imitate.—
The moon was calmly shedding her silver light on
every object; the azure vault above was studded
with a thousand starry gems, whose twinkling rays
diffused a splendour o'er the captivating scene
which seemed almost as fair and beautiful as
when it first came from the hands of its Creator.
Awed and charmed by the majesty and grandeur of
the prospect, I abandoned my mind to its reveries,
and permitted it, unchecked, to wing its lofty flight
to the distant and unexplored regions which lie in

the immeasurable wilds of ether. As I surveyed the spangled firmament, with its innumerable shining luminaries and planetary worlds, and reflected on the reports of philosophy, which come to us alike sanctioned by revelation and reason, my mind was completely lost in the immensity of its conceptions and the sublimity of its ideas.

"Consult with reason: reason will reply,
Each lucid point that glows in yonder sky
Informs a system in the boundless space,
And fills with glory its appointed place;
With beams unborrowed brightens other skies:
And worlds unknown with light and heat supplies."

"Could you soar beyond the moon," observes the pious and elegant Hervey, "and pass through all the planetary choir; could you wing your way to the highest apparent star, and take your stand on one of the loftiest pinnacles of heaven; you would, there, see other skies expanded; another sun distributing his inexhaustible beams by day; other stars that gild the horrors of the alternate night; and other, perhaps, nobler systems, established; established in unknown profusion through the boundless dimensions of space." With thoughts like these, I gazed again at the glittering heralds of their Maker's praise, and wrapt in the the holy feelings caught from the "moral emanation of the skies," my soul poured itself out in adoration of that Almighty Power which

"————resides above them all,
In Glory's unapproachable recess."

I felt a spark of that sacred fire which glowed in the bosom of Israel's royal Psalmist, and involuntarily exclaimed, "O Lord! how great are thy works! In wisdom hast thou made them all; the heavens declare thy glory, and the firmament sheweth thy handy work."

There is something unspeakably grand in the contemplation of the starry heavens:——nothing tends to open the mind to more elevated, and fill it with more worthy thoughts. The solemn season of the night is especially fitted for pious and exalted musings; silence and solitude concur to hush our passions, soothe our feelings, and invite us to deep and serious, though not melancholy, thought.——Contracted must be the mind, and cold the heart, that can then find nothing to awaken its present imaginings;—low and grovelling must that soul be, indeed, that it cannot, at least, for a season, allure from the ordinary, business thoughts of life; in which it cannot allay the fervour of human passions and human anxieties, and exalt it above the little competitions, factions, and debates of mankind, to the enjoyment of nobler and more refined speculations. At such moments, with what commanding majesty does *Religion* strike the well instructed mind! The sceptic *may* sneer; the infidel *may* scoff: I heed not their empty pride or scorn: they pass by me as the wind which idly raves around the head of the forest's towering oak. Firmly founded on the Christian's faith, and happy in his bright hope and vision of immortality, I can smile at their puny efforts to shake a confidence, which rests upon the eternal *Rock of ages.*—Christianity has nothing to fear from investigation; she dreads no ordeal, however severe, by which her claims upon our reverence and belief may be tested: she courts the light of the torch of science and truth; and it is delightful to reflect that many of the most distinguished ornaments of the world, the most illustrious characters in the ranks of wisdom and learning,

B*

have thought it their highest honour and greatest
happiness to sit meekly at the feet of Him who
"spake as never man spake," and learn from those
lips, which ever breathed but benevolence and love·
With a genius touched by the hallowed fire of Re‾
ligion, their talents derived from it their purest
nourishment and noblest elevation. And will the
pigmy witlings of the present generation pretend
to pierce farther into the depths of evidence and
reason than did the acute, the penetrating, the
giant minds of those who were the boast and glory
of their age; whose discoveries have inscribed their
names in imperishable characters on the scroll of
fame, and whose memories will be cherished to the
end of time, as the greatest benefactors of mankind? Rather let them imitate them where alone
they can, and by a strong, steady, and masculine
piety, evince their trust in the Christian's God.——I
mean not that cold, lifeless, and insipid assent to the
great and solemn truths of revelation, which, as the
celebrated Addison remarks, may rather be called
philosophy than religion, "and leaves its professor
frozen at heart, while speculation shines;" but that
vivid principle of faith whose throne is the *heart*,

where it springs up as a never failing fountain of
life and peace, calling forth the sweetest enjoy-
ments, the purest refinements, and the most exquisite sensibilities of our nature.—Let them strive to
copy the bright example and emulate the christian
virtues which, dwelt in the pious and philosophical
bosom of him whose mighty genius first threw open
those vast fields of contemplation to be found in the
heavens, and whose venerable and illustrious
name will live as long as one of those planets whose
distance he measured, and whose magnitude he described, shall continue to roll in obedience to those
laws and principles he first discovered.—*Newton*
was a Philosopher; he was an Astronomer; above
all, he was a *Christian;* and often, I doubt not, has
his vast soul expanded with silent adoration as he
looked upon the magnificent wonders of the evening sky, and beheld the works of an Almighty
hand.—Let me follow him, at an humble distance,
and, like him, never blush to be found prostrate at
the footstool of that Being whose sceptre sways
universal nature, whose glory fills the universe, and
who hath left the footsteps of a God on every spot
throughout Creation's wide domain!

THE WRECKERS.

BY J. H. HEWITT.

"LET us go forth and look upon the sea,
Our babes are hush'd—though loud and mournfully
The wind begins to howl, yet, on they sleep,
The little innocents!—nor heed the deep
And hollow murmur of the waves, as o'er
The mossy rocks they plunge toward the shore.
Look—where the sad moon sets, her farewell ray
Kissing the wave-tops as she steals away;
While round her silver disc, swift gathering,
The heralds of the storm come on the wing
Of the mad north! And lo! that flash of light
Adding new horror to the dreadful night;—
And hear the mutt'ring of yon leaden cloud,
As threat'ning o'er the deep it hangs; while loud
The untamed winds rush from the turbid north
And bid the spirit of the storm come forth.

Come to the beach—I love to see the deep
Stirred by the wrath of heav'n, and lightnings leap
From bursting clouds—to watch the angry wave—
To hear the wild wind's and the sea-gull's stave;
Methinks I'm in the presence of my God,—
Whene'er I breast the storm, or on the flood
Raised by his mighty pow'r, I dare to gaze,
My heart bespeaks his love, my lips his praise.

See!—see! that glare, 'twas not the lightning's flash
Nor was that boom the doubling thunder's crash;
Again—again, now hear the wild halloo
From the loud trump above the tempest's hue,
Husband! come forth, for by the sheet of fire
That pours from yonder cloud of deadly ire,
I see a ship upon the reefs—her shrouds
Lined with the victims of the waves and clouds.
We have a brave boy on the sea—a child
Whom we did love most dear; and when he smiled
He was so like his father, that to me
The day was sad when he was sent to sea—
Alas!—alas! may God in mercy keep
The lov'd one from the dangers of the deep!"

Thus spake the mother, as upon the shore
Fearless she stood amid the tempest's roar,

Whilst through the leaden tapestry of heaven,
The wrathful fire and thunder-bolts were driven;
Wave upon wave leapt hissing toward the sky,
Split by the winds in their mad revelry;
And ever and anon, with vision strained,
She mark'd the shatter'd bark which still remained
Pent in by breakers, lash'd by every wave
That gaping shewed the mariner his grave.
The life-boat soon leapt from the pebbly shore,
Mann'd by the hardy and the brave; and o'er
The mountain surges danced, its only guide
The livid fires of heav'n.　On, on they plied
The sturdy oar,—oft down the liquid glen,
Or perched upon the frothy peak, and then
Whirled back upon the beach—In vain they strove,
The winds and waves before the clouds above
Warr'd 'gainst humanity, the ire of heaven
Was on the mighty deep—the boat was riven!

Now loud above the storm the wild shrieks swell
Of those on board the ship—it speaks too well
Her fate, a transient flash illumes the sea—
The waves roll madly on—but where is she?

Long watched the wreckers on the rocky shore,
The waves went down, the thunder growl'd no more;

Hush'd were the winds, the storm had pass'd away,
And in the saffron east the streaks of day
Came with the golden sun.   Where was the wreck?
No trace was left, save far away a speck
Of snowy white which on the sand was seen,
Like sea-foam left to catch the sunbeams' sheen—
Thither the mother sped—alas! for her,
Why did the deep refuse a sepulchre
For that dead boy?—she seized his icy hand,
Kiss'd his blue lips, half buried in the sand;
"My own lov'd boy!" she loudly shriek'd and wept,
As if her sobs would wake the one that slept;
No, he was cold,—his eye was fix'd and dim,
And storms and sunshine were alike to him!

MOONLIGHT.

BY T. C. ATKINSON.

THE moon rides high in heaven and each fair star
Like modesty that from the glare doth flee,
Retires serenely through the dome afar
And leaves heaven's concave one cerulean sea,
Waveless and free from breaker-rock or bar,
O'er which pale Dian courses silently,
Like a fair ship, or more, a queenly swan
Cleaving the silent wave of Mississawgaigon.*

Her beam hath paled the green of our alcove
And as it were a winding sheet hath bound;
Oh! is not the approach of death, my love,
Enfolding silently its victims round,
Like moonlight gently falling on a grove
And levelling its shadows to the ground?

* Lake Superior.

Our bodies are but shadows prostrate lying,
The soul still virid and its flowers undying.

Yet, love, there is a brilliance in this hour
That's not of moonlight; we'd forego the skies
And stars from their bright stations, and our dower
Should be the radiance of each other's eyes;
Though one thick cloud of endless night should lower
Above us and around us, there should rise
From out our hearts, a sympathetic flame
Guiding us on our way, unfalt'ring and the same.

Ah! what were worth the beauty of the soul?
Or who would seek to win the spirits light
Or long for loveliness and love's control,
If, when the sun hath set in lasting night,
The starry pageant of the midnight pole
Vanished away, for aye, from mortal sight,
It may not be translated to the skies
Unsevered from the heart, that won its earthly sighs?

Planets may whirl through chaos uncontrolled,
Stars from their courses sullenly retire,
Systems may play the rebel as of old
A single star did, and assail their sire

C

When the great death bell of the sun hath toll'd
Consumed upon his own funereal pyre,
The heavens may shrink and shrivel as a scroll
But love, triumphant love, shall overlive the whole!

THE DEAD BRIDE.

BY N. C. BROOKS.

———

THE moon's bright beams, like liquid silver pour
From her full orb, the opened casement through,
And shed their lustrous brilliancy upon
The face of sleeping beauty.   Zephyrs mild,
With lightsome wing, are fanning her soft cheeks,
And gently stir upon her snowy brow
The glossy ringlets of her raven hair.
The bride of Asman sleeps.

                Her dark blue eyes,
Are curtained from the sight by glossy folds
Of soft and silken fringe.   A placid smile
Oerspreads her features, and her rosy lips
Are sweetly parting, as if bliss too pure
For waking hours was gushing through her breast
In gentle tides of sweet ethereal joy.
So calm, so sweet, so silent her repose,
Her breathing is not heard; the gentle blood

Glides pulseless through her veins, and the drawn
     breath,
Heaves not her rounded bosom's snowy swell.
The bride of Asman's dead.
                Her calm repose
Is the still dreamless slumber of the grave.
Death's gloom is on her eyes; their snowy lids
Are closed to ope no more; and her pale brow
Has drear mortality's cold, icy chill,
And the sweet smile, her lovely features wear
The peaceful soul imparted, as it left
Its spotless shrine within her virtuous breast,
Giving her smiling lips th' ambrosial glow
Of heavenly life and immortality.
The bride's upon her bier.
                Wrapped in her shroud
Of long and snowy white, we seem to gaze
Upon a seraph of the upper spheres,
Reclining in her white and shining train.
On couch of pure and heavenly brightness,
Till the dark wreaths of cypress round her strew'd
The rending groans of Asman's bursting heart,
And the funereal tapers burning at her head
Confirm the mournful truth, the lovely Ada's dead.

THE STAR OF ST. PHILIPPE

Lith. of Endicott & Swett.

THE STAR OF ST. PHILIPPE.

BY CYPRIAN ORMOND.

"She was a form of life and light,
Which seen became a part of sight
And rose, where'er I turn'd mine eye,
The morning star of memory."

THE summer and fall of 18—— were noted by the oldest inhabitants of the City of New Orleans, as the most unhealthy season within their recollection.—— Even the acclimated did not uniformly escape the pestilence, which, during a pause of several comparatively healthful years, seemed to have been collecting its concentrated powers of desolation. A few days after the disease of the climate had given decided manifestations of its appearance, but had not yet spread widely enough to excite the public feeling, or awake the public voice, I strolled, as was my custom, about the dusk of evening to Mas-

C *

pero's coffee house, at the corner of Chartres and
Tholouse streets. The spacious apartment was
lighted by a splendid chandelier, suspended from
the centre of its lofty ceiling. At the upper end of
the room stood the elegantly ornamented bar, where
refreshments of every description awaited the call
of the customers. The walls were decorated with
paintings, engravings, and framed hand-bills of various kinds flourishing in fancy type. Every accom-
modation combined to render the room an agreeable resort to the merchants of the city.

This was the hour at which, after the light re-
past of the evening, they assembled to discuss the
politics and business of the day. Groups were collected near the doors and windows to catch the little
air that breathed through the streets, while others,
in spite of the stifling stagnation of the surrounding
atmosphere, were seated closely together in the interior of the apartment, disputing, with French vehemence of tongue and gesture. Over several small
tables bent couples engaged in the game of domino,
a pastime greatly in repute among the grave rem-
nants of the ancient dominion. Newspapers were
in the hands of many, and before the bar stood a

number of thirsty souls, sipping lemonade or claret, or awaiting the concoction of some favorite beverage. I joined them and called for a cup of coffee. Though a resident of New Orleans for the last seven years, I had never conformed to the custom of my neighbors, in changing my warm evening draught for a cool one, although I would perhaps have evinced better taste and sense by the substitution.

Having leisurely disposed of the contents of my cup, I passed from group to group, catching the current news of the day and commenting upon it. The subject of the fever was but slightly touched upon, for it disturbed not the minds of those, whom reiterated exposure to the contagion had sunk into apathetic disregard of its terrors.— After sauntering through the room, I paused before a painting whose beauties had often yielded me an enjoyment which increased by repetition. It was the Ariadne of Vanderlyne, reclining upon the sea-shore after Theseus relinquishing her to Bacchus, had left her slumbering upon the strand of Naxos. The contour and colour of the figure were faultless. She seemed lost in voluptuous visions of the hero who had left, or of the god to whom he had resigned, her. The soft placidity of the picture communicated its dreaming quietude to the gazer, and I became lost in delicious reverie, as I stood with folded arms before it—A tolerably smart tap on the shoulder aroused me, and turning, I discovered an individual whose appearance made me start with astonishment. "Gracious heaven!" I exclaimed, "are *you* here still: I thought you were at the Balize by this time."

The person whom I addressed was a young man, for whom I entertained the most affectionate friendship. His name was Augus Wallingford, I had known him as a boy in my native place, in New England. He was the only son of a man of wealth. His natural genius had been cultivated by a finished education. As the companions of his brilliant parts, he possessed the wildest enthusiasm and the warmest passions: yet, mingled with this rank exuberance of feeling, there was a lofty generosity of temper and elevation of character. Originality was his aim; yet his eccentricity was not the flightiness of the fool, conspicuous only for his absurdities.— In person he was eminently prepossessing, in age scarce three and twenty. After the conclusion of his studies, he determined to become a wanderer for a while. To his projects of peregrination his father reluctantly assented, wishing him the advantages of travel yet fearing to trust him out of his control. Augus might have gone at once to Europe; his father desired it; but he declared, that he would study his own country first, so that, when catechized by the people of other lands, he might not disgrace himself by ignorance of his own. Leaving his home about a year since, he had traversed nearly the whole of the Western States and, a couple of months back, had presented himself to me in New Orleans. He had arrived at manhood since I had last seen him. I soon saw, in his character, the mixture of faults and excellencies, which composed it, and attaching myself closely to him, endeavored to supply to him the want of a restraining friend.

I introduced him into the best society of the place, in which he made a brilliant figure. With his usual versatility, he caught at once the tone of the circles of fashion in which he moved. He became the favorite of his associates of both sexes and formed for them an equal predilection. Thus he had gone on, enjoying himself among a people whose man-

ners and mode of life he found pleasingly congenial
to his own notions. As the period drew near, when
the epidemic of the climate was to commence its ravages, I constantly urged upon him the necessity of
a timely withdrawal. · He promised to be ruled by
my advice, but declared that he would stay till the
last allowable moment and not be too easily frightened from so paradisaical a spot. Not until several
ases of yellow fever had occurred, of peculiar viru-
lence, could I persuade him to take passage in a
ship bound for Savannah.

Twenty-four hours ago, I had seen him on board,
and beheld the ship unmoor and fall down the river,
with a favorable breeze. What then was my astonishment to see him again at my side, when I was
congratulating him upon the distance that lay between us. To my expressions of surprise and regret, he replied laughingly, "upon my soul, a most
hospitable friend; I risk my life to see you once
again, and instead of feeling adequately grateful for
the visit, you wish me to my face an hundred miles
away; I will be more chary another time encoun-
tering the plague for the pleasure of your company."

"I trust you will, and would to God you had done so in this instance. But since you are here, explain I pray you how you got here!"

"Why that is soon done—We dropped down the river with a pretty breeze, but it died into a dead calm before we got half a dozen miles, and then it was a sluggish, loglike float to the English turn, where the stream takes a bend that seemed to be bringing us right back again, and that so slowly, that I thought I might as well quicken my course in the desired direction. So I made the captain just put me ashore and seizing a raw boned nag, I got hold of at a sugar plantation, I trotted up to town, promising to be back before the ship had travelled ten miles further. I arrived at the City Hotel just at two o'clock, and as I dismounted from my gallant steed, who should come up but my particular friend Walter Willis, who impressed and carried me off to dine with him, and here I am fresh from a bottle of celestial Burgundy." The flush upon his face confirmed this confession. Remonstrance upon the the madness of his conduct, especially in his present state of excitement, I knew to be useless. I

therefore merely asked, when he intended returning to the ship.

"Oh, so as to catch her somewhere between this
and the mouth of the river, my moveables and mo-
ney are snug in my trunk on board, and that, you
know, is security enough for my pursuing her. I
shall take an early start in the morning, lest a gale
should sweep suddenly down stream and carry my
chattles out to sea in a hurry."

"Yes," I remarked, "your situation, at this moment, is not unlike that of Ariadne here: her lover
has left her on shore, and is running away from her
as fast as he can, and so is your luggage treating
you, who are equally insensible to the abandon-
ment."

"A good parallel" he replied with vivacity, as he
fixed his eyes upon the painting. "What incompa-
rable loveliness in that form and face; stay, I have
discovered a resemblance in it to another than myself, yes a living, literal likeness to the most beauteous creature in creation, who first met those eyes
not an hour since. As I sat with Walter at our
wine, he suddenly called to me to look out of the
window; I ran to it and saw a lady passing, who at

that moment turned her face towards me and our eyes met; there was electricity in the encounter; such a countenance! I cannot describe it, but by its effects upon me and by pointing to the face before you, which, if those lids were lifted and the eyes they cover illuminated with the soul, that now slumbers beneath them, would give you a faithful idea of her whom I have seen. The resemblance in form is even more perfect than in face, for a shape so exquisitely moulded never moved upon the earth. Scarcely had she passed when I was all eager inquiry. Willis could only tell me that she had arrived yesterday, in the steam boat Tamerlane, from Louisville; that she was an actress, a star in all the splendors of its ascendant whom the manager of the St. Philippe Theatre had engaged for a short season, at an immense cost, that her parentage was highly respectable, her character dignified and spotless, her name Clara Wilton, and, lastly, that she was to play this very night, in the character of Juliet. You may be sure I did not long deliberate about going to see her, aud was on my way to the Theatre when I stept in here for a

D

glass of iced lemonade as a cooling counteractor of my wine."

He pulled out his watch, observed that he had ten minutes to spare, ordered the refrigerating draught, in which I consented to join him, and we sat down at a table, alternately to taste and talk.—My eye was at this moment attracted by an individual, who sat within a few feet of us, at a little stand on which was placed a cup of coffee, that remained untouched before him, though an inviting vapour curled upwards from its surface. He was a man considerably advanced in life, his head partially bald and his hair almost white; his countenance was clouded by settled care. I recollected to have seen him several times, within the last month or two, and to have marked him as a man of unusual appearance : but of his name and history I knew nothing, nor had curiosity even prompted me to inquire respecting them. My attention had been called to him at this moment by the regard he seemed to pay to us. The back of my friend being turned towards him, I was the only observer of this. He held a newspaper in his hand, but his eyes instead of resting upon it, looked over the spectacles he wore and were fastened upon me, in that steady gaze, which often rivets the sight upon an object of interest, with an influence like that of the snake upon the bird. When he found me reciprocating his stare, he resumed his reading, and as he withdrew his eyes a rapid change passed over his countenance, like the convulsion of mental pain. He put his coffee to his lips, but scarce moistened them, and in a few moments arose and left the room.— Augus seeing that I watched the motions of the old man, upon whom he bestowed a casual glance, asked who he was. "I cannot inform you," I said, "for he is, except by sight, utterly unknown to me; but he seems to have been affected in an extraordinary manner by something that has been said by one of us, most likely by yourself, for you have talked in a tolerably audible tone I assure you which I have been fifty times upon the eve of advising you to repress."

"Pshaw"—said he, "I never had a secret in my life and therefore I never whisper; but come, it is time to go; you will of course give me your company." I consented, although I was no play-goer, and had not even noticed the bill which hung from

the wall before me, and a glance at which now
showed me, its emblazoned lettering, the announcement of the lady, whom my friend was dragging
me to see and admire.

The theatre over which St. Philippe has the honor of presiding is a spacious and splendid structure of rich and tasteful architecture. It presented, at the moment we took our places, a spectacle
to dazzle and delight. The first seats of the first
and second range of boxes were filled by the beauty and fashion of the city, arrayed in its gayest ap-
parel, and, as if this semicircle of splendour were not
enough to fascinate the sight, a mirror curtain added to the circle its other half and doubled the
magnificence of the scene. As we seated ourselves,
the green curtain was on the rise, unfolding the
vast field of that polished surface, from which the
audience beheld itself reflected. You might discern the instantaneous effect produced by the holding up of the gigantick looking glass, in the readiness with which each female in the glittering ring
sought out her own image in the mass of forms before her, and bestowed upon it an approving smile.
But there was brief time for the pleasing self con-

templation.   The mirror vanished, with its visionary duplicate of the assembly, and Romeo and his
companions strolled forward upon the stage.——
Their acting was respectable, nothing more; it was
the expectation of something better than had been
seen for a long time, that had called the crowd
now filling the house to overflowing.   Devotion to
the drama, a prominent passion of the French and
infused by them into the American part of the
population, made them forget the stifling heat and
the infection, which floated through the air of the
town, and which a throng like this could not fail to
concentrate and bring into action.   At length, to
the infinite ecstacy of Augus, who had with difficulty restrained a certain itch for sibilation that affected the tip of his tongue, while the poor devils
were doing their best, the scene opened in which
Juliet first came forth.   A thunder of applause followed her appearance, in which my companion
joined so energetically with a loaded cane, that he
battered the box to pieces and transformed the bul-
let head of his stick, from a sphere to an irregular
polyhedron, by the force and number of his blows.
She answered this compliment by an acknowledg-
    D*

ing inclination, so full of modest gratitude and grace, that it was reiterated again and again. In this scene she had but little to say; but the delicacy of her faultless features, the chaste purity and glowing brilliancy of her complexion, unheightened by art, the ever varying expression of her face, full of intellect and sentiment. The exquisite symmetry of her form, clothed in the most tasteful and appropriate costume, the richness, melody and well tempered power of her tones, and the unaffected grace of her attitudes and gestures, all manifested themselves within the few moments she stood before the audience. The delight of Augus was delirious, and forced from me a confession, that his account of this fascinating being had not been even tinged with exaggeration. She retired, I turned to address a friend behind me, when I perceived in one corner of the box, the elderly person who had attracted my attention at Maspero's. He was bearing back into the shade, but I marked the rapidly succeeding changes of his countenance.—His first aspect was that of pleasure, nay, delight, as if he had fully partaken of the popular feeling, which was still expressing itself in plaudits. Then he compressed his lips and his brow became wrinkled with intense pain, and the frown and muscular distortion of fierce anger followed. He seemed convulsed for an instant with passion, till burying his head in his hands, his face was concealed from my view. I continued to regard him with the feelings of curious interest excited by the unaccountable mystery of his conduct, till he raised his head and resumed his first posture, folding his arms and smoothing his countenance into rigid sternness, as if wrought up to endure the torment which had distracted his mind and visage.

From this time I kept my eye upon him. The play went on. In the masquerade scene, Juliet was hailed with redoubled rapture. Then came the interview with Romeo from the balcony, in which, as the character which she sustained developed itself, she began to evince the perfection of her conception and execution. Romeo himself caught inspiration from his mistress and surpassed, his former self. "The dolt, the vulgar villain!" ejaculated Augus in my ear "even *his* dull grossness cannot help being roused and refined by her presence and her converse. Cupid be praised, she is now out of his reach; how it pleased me to see her recoil from his kiss; it makes me blaze with jealousy to see him pollute her with his touch."

"Wait" said I smiling, "until we get them both into the tomb of the Capulets; she cannot then avoid coming to close quarters." "My life on it," he exclaimed, "she will even then conduct herself with consummate delicacy; though I am on fire at the thought of what she must inevitably submit to." Just then she uttered a passage of unpassing tenderness, with all the witchery of fresh and girlish fondness, and the feelings of the audience burst forth in a long and loud expression of approbation, which drowned several of the following sentences. Augus was in an agony as he strove in vain to catch the tones of her silvery voice. He cursed the crowd of boisterous brawlers, as he called them, besought them to cease their savage yells, and hissed with all his might. The pit gentry, interpreting this as an expression of contempt for their idol, only clapped the more, roared 'turn him out' and assailed him with various missiles, which took effect upon his innocent neighbours, as well as himself.— I tried to drag him back into the box but he leaned over the front still farther, and by the wild vehemence of his manner, attracted the attention of Juliet herself, who, for an instant forgot her Romeo to fix her eyes upon the youth, whose figure among the audience was so conspicuous. She seemed in a moment to understand his motives and smiled in gentle approval of them, while by a motion of her hand and head she appeared to deprecate the efforts to which they led. He saw the smile, understood the gentle reproof, and retired behind me out of the sight of the people below, delighted with her notice and happy in shewing his devotion, by instant obedience.

His disappearance stilled the tumult, and it was now my care to prevent his proving the cause of its recurrence. I besought him not to suffer his admiration of a pretty actress to make him regardless of public exposure and ridicule. My exhortations were not needed. His manner had changed as by magic, when he received that token of grateful, yet admonishing recognition; he became as quiet as a lamb; and during the rest of the play remained absorbed in deep attention to every word and look of Juliet; the passionate intensity of his feelings exhi-

biting themselves alone in the workings of his countenance. As he had asserted, she managed her motions with such matchless and delicate dexterity as
to avoid the touch of Romeo without seeming to
shrink from it; her dignity, devoid of prudery and
stiffness, yet awed and repelled him, although his
countenance told how ready he would have been to
take advantage of a player's privilege. When the
tragedy of the drama commenced, the eyes of the
audience began to moisten, and, so powerful was
the pathos of her acting, that the melting mood extended itself to those least troubled with sensibility.
I had occasionally cast an eye upon the elderly
stranger behind me. His emotions increased each
moment and at the close of the last scene his sobs
were audible; he arose and hastened out of the box.
Amid the tears of all around him, Augus shed not
a drop. The fountain seemed dried up by the
burning heat of inward passion. He sighed frequently and heavily, and when the curtain fell he
asked me to leave the house, as she was not to appear in the afterpiece.

It was about eleven o'clock when we found ourselves in the street. The moon was at the full and

the air fresh, compared with the atmosphere we had left. We directed our steps, by a common impulse, towards the river, and walked for some minutes in silence. There had been a peculiarity in the emotions of my companion, which made his conduct the subject of some perplexity to me, to behold him play the madman; crazy with delight, would not have surprized me, for such was his wont; but here there had been alternate exhibitions of mental ecstacy and agony. I sought an explanation by inquiry. His reply was, "my feelings are almost inexplicable to myself. Had I seen her when in as soberly phlegmatic a mood as any temperament will allow I should have worshipped her at first sight—no wonder then that warmed with wine I should have acted the lunatic, as I did at first. Thus far my behaviour is easily accounted for. But, when she motioned to me from the balcony, a sensation came over me I cannot define.— Some spirit seemed to whisper a mysterious intimation, that I had seen and known and loved that being once before. I was sobered in an instant and my mind fell into a train of thought, full of vague and struggling recollections and sensations as I strove to identify the object before me with an image long cherished in my soul's inmost recesses. That identification I have not yet effected, but the *possibility* that those two beings should be the same, is full of all bitterness. I will explain this to you. It is the only *secret* I ever had. Almost in infancy, the passion of love was developed in my constitution. I had a thousand little "*liaisons*" with children of my own age. At twelve I became attached by a genuine affection to the only daughter of Mr. Dartmere to whom my father, his intimate friend, paid a visit at his residence near Boston.— She was a little angel in beauty, intelligence and heart. For several weeks I was her constant companion; we soon doated upon each other, and the separation, that followed, almost burst our young hearts with anguish. I never saw her afterwards, I never breathed my feelings to a human being; but believe me when I tell you, that the childish love of the boy, not yet in his teens, has influenced every action and pursuit of the man's existence. A presentiment that destiny would one day bring us together, has operated on me, up to this hour.— I might have sought her out and wooed, and per-

haps won her long since; but I felt as if she was
reserved for *me* alone, and experienced no uneasi-
ness from the fear of successful rivalry. At all
events I resolved to take my chance and not present myself to her until I had made myself worthy
of her; for I heard that she was growing up a para-
gon of personal loveliness, genius, accomplishments
and sweetness of temper, and I determined to be
as even with her, as my natural endowments would
permit. You think me a hair-brained youth and
so, abroad, I am, but you know not what intellectual labour I have spent and still spend upon my
improvement. On this errand I started upon my
wanderings, that when they were finished I might
lay the fruits of my toil and travel at her feet.—
Regarding her thus, imagine my sensations on fancying that I recognized her in the Juliet of to-night.
She, the pure untouched, enshrined saint of my visions of paradise, an *actress*, prostituting her talents,
discarding her delicacy, exposed to public view,
converted into public property, the associate of the
unprincipled and immoral, gracious God! the bare
chance that it is she, is too harrowing to my heart;
can I be deceived in her person? she has grown

E

from childhood to womanhood, since last I beheld her, but she has a nameless something, that stamps identity upon the image and that something tells me it must be she."

"Is her father alive" I said, as a suspicion flashed across my mind, "and are you acquainted with his person?"

"I have never heard of his death; I think, nay, I am sure I should recognize him, for I saw him but three or four years ago." By this time we had arrived upon the levee. The City, with its white stuccoed houses, lay on the interior of the high embankment, and the shipping, with its dark hulls and its forests of spars and rigging, upon the outside in equally profound repose. It was as bright as the sunshine of noon. The sea breeze, whose steady current came freshly up the river, wafted the musquitoes from the shore, gave us a pure reanimating atmosphere to breathe, and fanned the feverish brow of my companion, who opened his bosom to the cooling air. The stillness was now and then broken by the shrill, harsh creaking of the ungreased wheels of one of those water carts, that ply daily and nightly through the streets, piercing the tortu-

red ears of the stranger, till his hardened auricu-
lars become habituated to the sound. In the pauses of this melody came music, floating over the
waters, of a finely contrasted description. It was
the rude chaunt of some negroes returning down
the river to their master's plantation, and beguiling
the toil of their oars with a wild yet rich and well
harmonized chorus. We walked slowly along the
levee in silence, until I spoke to him of his return
to the ship.—"No," he replied, "I have now a tie
that binds me here; my doubts must be removed
before I leave this place: if my suspicions are
groundless, I shall have nothing to detain me; if
otherwise, Oh! I know not what I can do, yet I will
not depart without making an effort to reclaim her
from her lost condition."

Hitherto we had encountered no one in our walk,
but, opposite fort St. Charles, whose white walls
and green mounds lay in the moonlight, a stone's
cast to our left, we saw a man coming slowly up
the levee;—he approached us, I recognized the old
man, who had been the subject of my close obser-
vation, and with whom, some singular sympathy
seemed to connect us. I felt intensely interested

in satisfying my suspicions in relation to this strange individual. I requested Augus to scrutinize his face keenly as we passed him, and then managed to throw myself in his way, so as to bring us both to a halt, for a time long enough to afford my friend the desired apportunity of scanning the face of the stranger. The recognition I expected took place, and the mutual astonishment of both parties was inexpressible, when, in the clear moonlight, my companion discovered the features of the father of Miss Dartmore, and the old man more slowly recalled the countenance of the son of his friend. · When the first ejaculations of surprise were over and I had been introduced to Mr. Dartmore, Augus hurriedly asked him, "Is Miss Clara Wilton, the actress, your daughter?" "Yes," he replied with a groan that seemed to come from his inmost heart, "she is, too truly, my lost, unhappy, unworthy child."—"You do not then countenance her present profession—meeting you here, I had for an instant feared that she was pursuing it under your protection."—"God in heaven forbid," he exclaimed, "no—no—she adopted and adheres to it in defiance of my authority and my wishes, knowing my peace to be ruined, my heart to be broken, my life rendered miserable and precarious by her conduct." "And what in heaven's name led to this disgraceful dereliction of her duty to you and to herself?"

"The story is soon told. When she was a child of ten years, I took her to see the "Children in the Wood" as a reward for some good behaviour, which had particularly pleased me. On that cursed occasion were sown the seeds of a passion for dramatic performances, which sprung up and ripened with fearful rapidity. She had at the age of fifteen, read every play in the modern languages worth perusing. Some private theatricals, which I unwillingly encouraged, confirmed the bias of her mind. That she possessed eminent genius for the stage cannot be denied; but was it therefore incumbent on me to assent to her adoption of a discreditable profession, which I abhorred, and thus throw away upon a selfish world the treasure I had been hoarding for years; my only child? No: not if I had been assured that her talents and success would have procured her the fame of Siddons.—Knowing all this, she kept her projects profoundly secret, I indulged her unsuspectingly with constant visits to the theatre. About eight months since, one fatal night upon which she had gone thither, her companions returned in alarm without her.— I hurried in quest of her, still blind to the dreadful truth; but I neither discovered nor heard of her, till her announcement a week afterwards to appear upon the New York boards, under the assumed name she now bears. When I recovered from the insanity to which the shock of this intelligence drove me, a spirit took possession of my soul which quelled the disposition to hurry after and reclaim her by persuasion or force. I said let her go. For five months I shut myself up from the world: the sympathy and condolence of my nearest friends were heart sickening to me. Confinement, however, become intolerable to my restless misery. I came hither, for the spot was remote from the home I could not endure, and its climate was one, whose pestilential terrors I courted rather than shunned; for of what value is life to one bereaved as I am? Little did I expect to be followed here by her.— When I learned she was to appear to night my rooted indignation struggled vainly against a parent's pride in the beauty, genius and attractions of his child and my feet bore me involuntarily to the house, where I was to behold her in that character, her assumption of which was the cause of all my misery. While she stood before me, the agonizing conflict of a thousand opposing emotions, wholly unmanned me. The perfection of her performance would sometimes beguile me into forgetfulness of the sad reality, and I, alternately, shared in the feelings of my fellow spectators, and became absorbed in those peculiarly my own. Often did I strive to break the spell, that bound me to my seat; but an enchanting infatuation kept me fast. My weakness in seeking the sight of my unworthy offspring, is the subject of self-exasperation and reproach. We never meet again."

"Say not so," earnestly exclaimed Augus, "but rather that you will delay not a moment in those endeavours to bring her back to you, which if made in season might have, nay I could swear would, have been assuredly successful."—"No," replied the old man, his features fixing themselves in stern inflexibility, "my resolves are not thus wavering; they are the fruits of a long and agonizing struggle between the weakness of natural affection and the strength of proud and high principled duty to myself; let her know the difference between the parent, whom she has abandoned to hopeless wretchedness, and the world upon which she has voluntarily cast herself." "Then," said Augus, "I must enter upon the work unaided and alone."—— "*You*," said the old man with incredulous emphasis, "*you* attempt her disengagement from her present career, what motives have you, if she is nought to *me* now, what can she be to *you*?"—— "Every thing," he answered, "have you forgotten how when children we idolized each other? Since childhood I have never beheld her; but she has ever been before my eye in anticipation and in soul my wife. Her present conduct and condition are therefore to me the sources of affliction and shame scarce inferior to your own. But her value is undiminished in my view, for I believe her still as innocent as when she left your roof; and that an infatuating delusion of the fancy has made her what she is. I cannot yet relinquish the hope of realizing that happiness with her, to which I have for years looked forward." The father slightly shook his head. "Your expectations of reforming a disobedient child are vain. She is no more my daughter. I have no interest in aught, that concerns her. Do what you deem fit. I believe your intentions towards her to be good and honorable; but, were they otherwise, I should not call you to account for them. She has thrown herself open to the libertine and joined herself to the profligate, and what is it to me to whom she falls a prey? would that I could banish her existence from my mind. I must leave you now. This place will not contain me long. I must fly from her as she once fled from me."

Further remonstrance was manifestly useless.— We offered to accompany him to his residence, but he declined our proposal and left us while we returned together to my own house. As we parted for the night, I said to Augus, "God speed your plans; command my aid in their execution. Above all be quick, that you may escape hence for I tremble hourly for you and for her also. Draw on me for whatever the absence of your baggage may render essential."

"What has your consultation with your pillow suggested," I inquired when we met in the morning; "in a matter of feeling like this I leave you to your own counsel."

"All that I have determined upon," he replied, "is to obtain an interview; I have not framed one argument to be urged, one persuasion to be employed, one sentence to be uttered; I cast myself upon her heart, and those impassioned impulses, which will excite me in her presence." He restlessly awaited the proper hour for his visit and then inquired his way to her lodging, a respectable boarding house in St. Anne street. He thus described afterwards to me what followed. "I awaited her appearance, with a throbbing heart and a whirling brain. Yet the occasion called for consummate management and self command. In what character should I address her? I could not declare myself her father's delegate, for he had disowned her. I must act upon my own responsibility, and brave the reproach of impertinent interference with her actions. Should I remonstrate with her as a friend, or plead with her as a lover? My childish affection for her had been warmly reciprocated, but maturity seldom retains the traces of infantile feeling and, in speaking to her in the lan-

guage of passion I ran a fearful risk of contemptu-
ous repulse. Further reflection was cut short by
her appearance. What a vision of beauty burst
upon my sight; how unlike those of her profession,
who look like angels on the stage and withered
witches off of it. Attired with all the toilette's
trickery, and acting for applause in every look, she
dazzled the sense; but habited, as now, in modest
white with a single rose among the clustering ringlets on her temples and her neck, she melted the
soul. I saw before me the matured image of my
boyish love. I arose trembling in every nerve; I
opened my lips without the power of articulation;
her eyes sunk under my regard and her face became suffused with crimson. The intense struggle
of an instant then enabled me to say, "I cannot
apologize with sufficient humility for this intrusion,
the object of which I fear I shall be as little able
to justify in your eyes; but before I name myself,
will you indulge me by one effort to recollect, in
me, an old acquaintance." The rapid recovery of
her self possession bespoke the presence of mind,
her avocations had already given her. The earnest,
yet modest scrutiny of a moment, seemed to awak-

en her recollections. "I seldom forget a face I
have once thoroughly known," she said with charm-
ing frankness, "through the lapse of many years and
your change from the boy to the man, I still recognize you as Augus Wallingford, the companion of
some of the happiest hours of my childhood. I
must then," she added with a playful air, "acknow-
ledge your claims to acquaintanceship." She met
my proffered hand. The pressure was to me delicious. We seated ourselves, and after a moment's
silence, I mastered my thoughts and words suffi-
ciently to enter upon my delicate subject. I remarked upon the strange coincidence of our meeting in this distant place. I spoke of the danger she
incurred and conjured her to fly from it. As I proceeded, the ardor of my feelings, fed by the fuel
of her glowing beauty, hurried me on to that, from
the mention of which I had at first shrunk. I recalled the period of our early intimacy, and assured
her that the childish fondness of infancy had ripened into the matured affection of manhood. I told her
of my hopes long cherished though, till now, unre-
vealed, and I besought her not to blast, but to bless
them, by consenting to exchange her present fatal

though fascinating career, for one in which happiness of a purer, better sort would become the portion of us both.

She listened with a changing countenance, from whose fluctuations I alternately gathered good and evil omens. At length I paused, when rising she replied with dignity, "I would consider your allusions to that profession, I have from choice adopted, as an unwarrantable interference with that which concerns myself alone, did not the sentiments and intentions with which you honor me absolve you from the censure of impertinent officiousness; of the feelings, with which your abrupt declaration of those sentiments have inspired me, I must be pardoned for saying more than that I am truly grateful for your flattering estimate of myself and your interest in my, welfare." She retired before I could say another word. For a moment I reproached myself for not urging my solicitations by a disclosure of her father's unhappy situation; but the hope and pride of being the sole instrument in the change I am striving to effect, have determined me to reserve this argument until the last. And now tell me what think you of my chance." I talked to him encouragingly, for I thought his enterprize commendable, and, gifted as he was with such recommendations to her favor, by no means desperate. On the following morning he sought her abode again and returned to me with countenance brightening with hope.

"She obstinately adheres," he said "to her profession; but it is becoming more delightfully apparent each moment, that time and absence have failed to eradicate the seed sown in childhood and whose germ now warmed by the presence and the passions of its object is budding into life and luxuriance. This is no conceit of my vanity, no suggestion of deceiving hope, and to the operation of these hourly strenghtening feelings I look for the full consummation of my wishes. She is announced to night, as Ophelia. You will go?"

We went at an early hour. The house was more thronged than before. I never witnessed such perfection in the personification of character, and I half excused her for the adoption of a profession she so splendidly adorned. I caught a glimpse of her father, in a remote corner of the house. A resistless impulse drew him thither, in spite of every struggle against it. He disappeared the instant she retired. Two or three days now went by, during which the visits of Augus to his mistress were of increasing frequency. His devotion to her became of course the public talk, and, as the favorite of the lovely actress, he was subjected to the envy and the banter of his old companions. But he soon stopped their rallying, little replete as it was with respect to the woman, he adored. In her affections he made rapid advances; but she still unyieldingly refused to retire from the stage and declared her determination to fulfil her engagement with the manager, though at the expense of her life.

The yellow fever had commenced its fearful march of devastation and the number of its victims increased with each succeeding day. On Saturday night she was to sustain the part of Desdemona.— The progress of the plague seemed to pass unnoticed by the inhabitants, who crowded to behold her. At the commencement she exhibited her usual spirit and power, but after some time animation seemed to leave her; her countenance grew languid, her voice trembled and her motions became slow and laborious. "She is ill," whispered Augus to

me, "she is ill, she must not go on." I remarked, that it might be oppression arising from
the extreme heat, and begged him to be calm. After sustaining herself until the death scene by the
most toilsome exertion, she sunk fainting upon the
couch prepared for her. Her companions thronged from behind the scenes and surrounded her.—
The house was confusion and uproar, and the people, after expressing, in every variety of voice,
their pity and disappointment, soon dispersed. Augus, leaping from the second tier of boxes upon the
stage, was in a moment at her side. I ran for a
carriage, in which, with her lover and a female as-
sistant, she was conveyed in a state of insensibility
to her lodging. A physician was soon procured,
who pronounced her to be in a high fever. I saw
how it was, and groaned over the probable result.
Her great efforts had exhausted her at the commencement of the disease and took away so much
of the strength, which a struggle with it demanded.
Augus was in an agony of alarm, he refused to go
home with me, declaring he would not quit the
house in which he was for an instant. As I left the
house, I passed a person standing near the door.—

It was the father of the patient. In a voice choked with emotion he inquired the situation of his daughter. Poor old man! thought I, nature is too strong within you for this assumption of cruel indifference to the fate of your child. I told him my apprehensions. He shuddered and turned from me; he never moved more than a few steps from the door the livelong night. Augus who had passed the hours in pacing one of the lower apartments, opened the door for me in the morning with a haggard countenance. She was now delirous and the awful crisis was hastening onward. But I pass over these details of bodily suffering and mental misery, which rendered the two following days so fraught with wretchedness to those interested in the event.

On the evening of the second day Clara Dartmore breathed her last, I tore my unhappy friend from the abode of death and forced him home with me. He had neither eaten nor slept for forty eight hours and the fever was now upon *him* too; "another victim," I said "as I beheld the verification of my fears and predictions approaching; the same grave will hold you both, and there all chance of separation will cease

H*

where you are unconscious of the consummation of that eternal union you have desired. Augus however was perfectly himself, though the infection had marked him for its own. He gave no outward exhibition of grief, and seeming to yield to my entreaties that he would seek his bed and submit himself to the treatment of the physician for whom I had sent, he begged me to hasten back to St. Anne street and see that the last offices were performed; wishing to gratify him in every thing, I went. The intense heat of the weather made immediate interment necessary. I found the preparations for the burial of Clara going on, and that she was to be consigned to the tomb in a few hours. The family among whom she had resided were rigid Catholics and, wishing the funeral service of their own church to be performed over the deceased, they had determined to carry her body to the Cathedral church, previous to its deposit in the earth; I could make no objection to this arrangement. A little after eleven all was ready, the coffin palled and placed upon its bier, and with three other young men of the neighbourhood, I assisted in bearing it along. The night was without a star, a priest with his cross and book preceded the small though solemn procession, and three torch bearers

lighted our steps through the narrow and shadowy
streets. Far behind me in the darkness, a moan of
anguish occasionally interrupted the sad stillness of
the scene. It came from the miserable parent who
bewailed in death the daughter he had implacably
refused to forgive in life; we arrived at the Cathedral and entered through a small door, near the Sacristy. The spacious edifice was illuminated but
by our torches, and a few dim candles upon one of
the smaller altars. These lights dispelled the gloom
immediately around us, touched with a dull lustre
the ornaments of the chancel and gave back a faint
far gleam from the gilded organ, which reposed untouched and silent in the distant gallery. But a
vast canopy of sombre shadow, expanding its dusky
wings, floated heavily over the aisles and their melancholy occupants; the bier was set down before
the altar, the pall removed, the yet unfastened lid
of the coffin taken off and the shrouded form of its
lovely and lamented tenant was displayed.

We stood on either side awaiting the appearance
of the officiating priests, who in a few minutes came
forth from the sacristy in the sacred vestments of
their office. We sunk upon our knees as they advanc-

ed. Père Antoine, the venerable pastor of the parish church, commenced the burial service. He was an aged man of diminutive frame, attenuated features, and a countenance replete with benevolence; a small black cap covered his head on whose temples a few grey hairs appeared, like the last leaves of autumn foliage. His voice was soft and clear, though slightly trembling with the feebleness of years, and his words came sadly articulate to the 'ear in the rich music of the Latin tongue, while the deep, bass tones of the responding priests contrasted the mild tenor of his own. When the last amen was breathed and the lid of the coffin was about to be replaced, the heart broken parent came forward from his concealment. "Shut her not up for ever," he said, "till I have made my peace with my poor child. While you lived my daughter your were dead to me, but death has restored you to me alive again. This kiss of reconciliation is the token that we shall soon be united never more to be separated or estranged." "Alas my son," said the excellant Père Antoine as a tear stole from his eye, "is this a moment for forgiving those who have wronged us, and could you thus postpone the pardon of your erring child.

Of what avail is your forgiveness to her now, when perhaps she expired under the horrors of your curse." "No, old man, my daughter I could never curse, though she merited the anathema, but I did worse, I abandoned her to the evil way she had chosen; oh, if it were not now too, too late, whither would I not go, what would I not do to seek and save thee my poor wanderer."—He wrung his hands in agonized anguish. "It is indeed too late, my son," resumed the father, you cannot revive the spiritless clay before you, it is our duty to return it to its kindred ashes; we respect your grief and cannot interfere with its indulgence; but for your own sake, we would ask you to retire to your closet and the consolations of your religion, while we proceed to the fulfilment of our melancholy office."— "Perform your duty" said the unhappy parent turning away, "my eyes have taken their last look of her, and may *they* now speedily close in darkness."

The lid of the coffin was now fitted on its place, and the first screw that was to fasten it down had been several times turned, when a noise was heard at the door by which we had entered, and Augus rushed into the church. He stared for a moment

wildly around him, then staggered towards the bier,
and seizing the hand of the man who was engaged
at the coffin, with one effort of delirious strength
tore the plank from the place, to which it was already partially attached; I stepped forward to prevent this act of insanity, but he shook me off and
snatching the hand of Clara, which reposed by her
side, pressed it convulsively between his own, held
it to his heart as if to warm by its burnings the cold
flesh of the corpse, and leaning over the pale face
covered it with kisses. He panted for breath, for
he had flown to the place and the raging fever which
had seized him scarce left him strength to reach it.
At length he gasped out. "She is not dead, I dreamed that she was dead, but I have now awaked from
the horrible vision. See there is life, there is motion here, believe me, she is not, she cannot be dead."
He sunk senseless upon the body. I raised him,
but as I bent over the coffin, gracious God! what a
sight presented itself. He had spoken the truth.
The eyes of Clara were wide open; her lips were
parting; her bosom heaving; her form trembling
with nervous life. She was not dead in truth. I
saw the course instantly to be pursued, vitality

almost extinguished, had yet slumbered in her sys-
tom, and this was the moment of reaction.   I called for wine.   There was some in the sacristy,
which the excellent old priest hesitated not to divert from its holy purpose to one not less sacred.
A portion of it revived her sensibly, she was placed
in a carriage, still unconscious of outward objects,
and once more laid upon the bed, from which she
had been conveyed to the grave.   The fever had
exhausted itself upon her and the natural energies
had now only to be stimulated.   Augus was taken
to my house.   The disease now fairly pervaded his
blood and for days I despaired of his life.   But a
vigorous constitution bore him through and he recovered.   Clara's father never left her.   When
consciousness and memory restored, showed her
her father acting as her nurse, the surprise and the
shame of meeting him shocked her severely; and
the violence of her emotions, and the bitter expression of her remorse, almost overwhelmed her feeble frame.   In the amnesty for all past offences
which he freely granted her, she found relief and
consolation, and at length enjoyed without alloy the
delight inspired by his presence and his care.   In a

fortnight the lovers mutually tasted the reviving cordial of a meeting. "I feel" said Clara when her father and her lover enquired if she would insist upon returning to the stage, "I feel like one who has accidentally swallowed some nauseous dose, mingled with food, of which he was extravagantly fond; but which he ever afterwards regards with loathing. My appetite for the drama was morbid and usatiable; but the incidents which have just occurred, are like the potion smothered in the sweets; they have made me look upon the stage with abhorrence."

"You know" said Augus to me one day "that I aim at originality in every thing, and, therefore, my present odd notion will not surprise you. Clara, with her father's approbation has consented to an immediate union; a thing on many accounts desirable; now my freak is, to be married by the old priest, who performed the burial service over my dear Clara, and at the very same altar. The hour to be sure shall be evening not midnight. The association of ideas will be rich and original, and give a spice of variety to the monotony of the matrimonial ceremony. Besides I hear the old fellow displayed great good feeling at the burial scene, and I feel quite attached to him, we are neither of us Catholics, but if she objects on that score we can easily employ another clergyman afterwards."— Augus had the management to arrange the matter to his fancy. I was present at the bridal and it must be confessed that the comparison of the present scene with the past produced a vivid effect. The benevolent face of Père Antoine lighted with a smile of pleasure as he dismissed them with his bénedicite. "My children go now in peace; the giver of all good hath brought you back from the gates of death to the enjoyment of all life's blessings; be never failing then in gratitude to him and in love to each other; and be assured, that you will ever hold a place in the thoughts and prayers of the old man, who now addresses you, not only for the brief remnant of his mortal life, but in that better world, to which he humbly hopes for a speedy translation." A few days after I saw the happy trio safely embarked for their home in the north. "Now" said Augus as he shook me by the hand for the last time, "now I will go in chase of my runaway baggage."

THE SUTTEE,

ON THE BANKS OF THE GANGES.

BY EDRED.

The clouds are sleeping in the far off west,
Like giant kings of gold, on purple beds,
Lulled by the purest minstrelsy of heaven.
The sun hath set, and the yet trembling wave
Gleams with its parting legacy of light;
The air is full of fragrance, for the stream's
Green shore is clad with flowers to the brink,
That seem to kiss the stealthy liquid wave
And drink fresh life from every new embrace.
The moon, pale regent of the night, now o'er
The eastern sky with swiftest haste its beams
Of mellow light outpours, as if no night
Should ever shadow o'er such sacred scenes.
Silence hangs on its leaden wing and breathes
Oppressive dullness, round, save at yon pyre,
That casts its cloud-like shadow o'er the flood,

And palls the beauties of the sunset skies.

*　　　*　　　*,　　　*　　　*

————————The wife hath bathed;
But ere she leaps upon the fatal pile
That soon will ope its fiery lips to bid
Dire welcome to the dark eyed girl, methinks
I hear her say: "Well it is o'er,—the dream,—
The golden pageant of my life—the scheme
Of pleasure piled on many a fragile hope
Of. dalliance in the fields of fantasie!
'Tis o'er,—and I behold yon dying orb
Kiss, ere he sinks into his azure grave,
The wide and heaving main; e'en so I gaze
With tranquil eye upon the fairy scene,
The green clad grove—yon dancing rill,
Whilst dreams of pleasure from my waning eye
Still gild them all nor make this death a wo!
Ah Oran! art thou here? no—'tis a shade
The phantom of the past,—th' undrained drop
That glitters in life's golden cup—and clings
With tenfold strength to its last hold! I haste—
I haste—to greet thee in the world of shades."

And hark—she sings! her liquid tones how like
The breezes of the sunny south, that bear

The roses' fragrant breath upon th' Æolian
   Harp, mingling perfume and song!

"I've gazed my last on my father's halls,
   I've touched the last string of my long loved
      lute,
But I cherish the fate that calls me away;
   Oh! I sigh not—I sigh not—I'm mute—I'm mute.

"Can a Hindoo look o'er these rosy plains
   And the skies all clad in their golden hues
Nor weep that she leaves them in beauty and youth?
   Oh yes—Oh yes—when heaven she views!

"The loveliest music that flew to my ear,
   Winged with the perfume of early flowers,—
Can win me no more to this glowing world,
   Or woo me to wish for happier hours.

"My parents lip wears no lure to recall,
   The eye of my infant no talisman hath,
Oh! nought in the hall on the hill or the grove
   Can steal me away from my shadowy path.

"Then on to the peace of the blessed above
   In the realms of the sun and the golden strung
      lyre—

Fare ye well—fare ye well!   I rush to my grave,
  I'll clasp thee my ———"

Th' unfinished line still clinging to her lip—
With one light bound the dark eyed phrenzied girl
Gains the pale body of her ancient lord—
And strains it to her breast.   Strange ecstacy!
Even he who bore the fatal torch, that was
To fling a blazing life into the pile
Astounded stood.

       "Why come ye not—on!—on!"'
The while her dark eye flashing, and her curls
Of raven blackness flaunting on the breeze
Like darkly streaming clouds of thunder drift,
Down—down upon her knees she fell, seeming,
With stretched arms and close clasp'd hands to beg
The Hindoo bride's dread death.

       ———Alas—tis done!

A monumental pillar of black smoke o'erhangs
The fatal spot, and mingles with the clouds,
I see no wife—no lord—nor do I hear
Some faint yet silvery tones of agony
Stealing like arrows on the drowsy air;—

  G*

There stands her parent, with undaunted eye,
No tear bedews his dark and hardened cheek,
No quivering lip betrays his mournful heart;—
For he dreams that she sleeps in some glittering
     star!

    *   *   *   *   *

Hark! hark the dreadful voice of Heaven in wrath,
Muttering its stormy threatnings o'er this sin!
The tempest is abroad—and strange winged sounds
Come bellowing by—and airy trumpets too—
And flashing blazes of blue, flickering flame
Do stream with more than eagle-strength along—
And deep toned thunder—and loud beating rain
Like that, which fell on Moses' sheltering ark;—
The spirit of the storm outspreads his wings
And shadowing o'er the Indian's early grave
Screams a wild dirge to mark her funeral hour.

LINES TO THE MEMORY OF

EDWARD C. PINCKNEY.

A Poet, whose hand held the divining rod of the affections
and brought to light the fountains of feeling wherever their
hidden waters flowed.

Once more, sweet spring, the gentle queen of flow'rs
Hath shook her pinions o'er this clime of ours,
And wrapt in southern fragrancy, she brings
Life in her breath and "healing on her wings."

The streamlets now in milder murmurs flow,
And flocks secure their ancient pastures know,
Her halcyon garments earth assumes again
And mild blue heavens attest the balmy reign.

But 'midst this scene and season of delight,
So rife with all that's beautiful and bright,
That pain and sorrow seem forbidden here
And death a dweller in another sphere,
From all that glads the heart, we're called to turn
And pour our sorrows over Pinckney's urn.

The strain of "beauty" shall no more be sung,
The lyre of "Italy" remains unstrung,
Sealed is the fount from whence their music flowed,
Gone is the minstrel to his long abode,
That eye which shone with intellectual fire—
That form whose bearing seem'd to breathe—Aspire!
That eye hath closed in everlasting night—
That form hath fallen from its lofty height—
That voice, once like the nightingale's, is mute,
And like the nightingale, he perished by the lute.
Boast of his friends, his country's rising pride,
He trod in Glory's vestibule—and died.

Around his brow all hands the laurel twined,
His fame ascended as his strength declined.
Still as he sung his melancholy lay,
His eye was lit with an unearthly ray,
Presaging him that early sacrifice,
Which aye awaits the fav'rites of the skies.

All poets have dominions of their own
Where reason cow'rs and fancy fills the throne.
To these retreats he loved to make repair,
When worn with life and life-consuming care.

In intellectual Arcady reclined,
He scans the beauteuous visions of his mind,
There broad savannas spread before his eyes,
At either end commingling with the skies,
Far in the front 'twixt earth and heaven he sees
The all-enclosing wave,—a gentle breeze
Dimple's the oceans cheek and o'er its isles,
A long, unvarying, fadeless summer smiles.
Seasons for him their circling change forego,—
His cloudless heavens no interruption know,—
The pure and perfect day—the peerless night—
Alternate with Latona's offspring bright—
Infinity of intermingling light!

Late was the hour, when for the Muses' lore
The gloom of midnight overhung our shore,
No solitary star of worth was seen
To cheer the longing vision with its sheen.
Oft did the gazer lift a wistful eye
In hope some nascent twinkler to descry
And oft with disappointment turn aside
To find the heavenly visitant denied.
At length, like spangles in the vast expanse,
Some faint and flickering lights were seen to glance,

Then gradually growing clear and bright
And others bursting momently to sight,
The heavens seem'd all a glow when Pinckney's star
Arose and threw its brilliancy afar.
First of his nation in the line of song,
What lofty honors to his name belong!
Like Phosphor flaming in the brow of dawn
He leads the train of kindling glory on,
Yet not like him to dwindle and decay
Before the full meridian blaze of day,
But hourly brightening in his upward march
Till gain'd the keystone of the azure arch.
There at his culmination shall he stand,
The beacon and the glory of the land,
Casting his radiance on his country's page,
The light of song through many a coming age.

Spirit of Pinckney! from that starry dome
Where minds like thine find their immortal home,
Oh! that I could inhale that soul of fire
Which thrill'd the living fibre of thy lyre,
Yet as I may not win such lofty aim,
Vouchsafe a kindly glance nor yet desclaim
These flowers by one upon thy memory shed,
Who loved thee living and laments thee dead.
May, 1828.   W. A. M.

THE RESURRECTION.

Night's, ebon banner floated o'er the world,
Nor moon nor star beamed through the sable robes
Of woe, that shrouded up the mourning sky,
And silence brooded o'er the sick'ning scene.
A martial band reclined upon their spears
In mute assemblage round Iesus' tomb
With watching they were wearied and soft sleep
       began
To steal with drowsy weight, upon their eyes;
When two long trails like fiery comets streamed
Athwart the darkness of the starless sky,
And a quick sound like rushing wings was heard,
Stirring the stillness of the sluggish air.
Near and more near blazed the resplendent orbs,
While chilling fear drove back the hurried blood,
In icy chillness to their throbbing breasts,
Till heaven's full glory burst upon their sight,
And flashed in fire reflected from their spears,
And wings angelic waving o'er their heads,

Two cherubs bright in Heavens effulgent rays,
Descended, furled up their pinions bright,
And stood beside the tomb of Zion's king,
They touched the ponderous stone that closed the
          tomb;
Backward it rolled obedient to the touch,
And gave to life the prisoner of death.
From out the gloomy portal of the grave,
Arrayed in his sepulchral robes of white,
Triumphant came th' Almighty King, who led
Captive captivity.   His countenance
Was mild as when he smiles upon the storm,
And the wild rage of warring Heaven serenes.
The eye of him that pierced him quail'd; the knees
Of the stout soldiers each the other smote,
And like men dead upon the ground, they fell.
Loud through his hollow caverns, murmured Death.
Dire wailings filled th' infernal regions wide;
While with triumphant hallelujahs rung
The joyous courts of high empyrean Heaven.

                              D———.

THE ENCHANTED GROTTO.

Lith. of Endicott & Swett

THE ENCHANTED GROTTO.

BY CARLIN LAMOEN.

"Imagination waves her fairy wand;
The spirits of the mould'ring dead come forth,
The crumbled fane, the column and the arch
Arise, and with redoubled splendour shine."

TASSO.

PASSING through a long tract of country diversified with the ruins of stately cities and temples, o'er whose walls the ploughshare of desolation had been driven, many of which have passed away and left not even a name behind them in the records of Antiquity, I came to Heliopolis, the city of the Sun as its name indicates, so renowned for its magnificent temple dedicated to Apollo. As I contemplated its dilapidated walls covered with the scurf of time, its magnificent fluted pillars, its colonnades of stucco and marble and numerous friezes of men,

H

beasts, birds, fishes and flowers, I noticed an octagonal column, which from its hieroglyphics I soon perceived had been dedicated to the Phœnix.*

I felt much interested in the discovery I had made and being anxious to learn all I could respecting this remarkable bird, began decyphering the hieroglyphics with the utmost care; and after some calculation, discovered that the five hundred years had elapsed since the appearance of the last, and that consequently the Phœnix must shortly appear. Elated with this further discovery I burst into an exclamation of delight, and expressed a wish that I might be so fortunate as to get a sight of the extraordinary bird. As I finished speaking I found at my side a person of antique and venerable appearance. His looks were gray, and his long white beard flowed upon his breast. In his hand he held a large scroll. His eye was not dimmed with age, but beamed with a mild expression of calmness and intelligence. Addressing me with a strange kind of familiarity, "follow me" said he "and thy wishes shall be gratified." Supposing him to be a priest, who, attached to the imposing splendors of

* Vide, Herodot.

the temple, had made a faithful representation of the same, with all ;its sacred appurtenances, I followed him, after instructing my guide to await my return at the ruin.

We proceeded down a little valley whose sloping sides were covered with date trees, and cocoa and tall cedars, interspersed with shrubbery that exhaling their delicious sweets filled the air with a profusion of perfume. Twilight had spread her gray mantle over the earth and threw a solemnity over the feelings, as we reached the bottom of the vale. The mouth of a dark cave there presented itself into which my conductor immediately entered. I followed with a mixture of awe and fear, which was heightened by the solemn echo of our footsteps, as they sounded through the reverberating cavern. The floor and sides consisted of layers of smooth stones, as evenly disposed, as if they had been the effect of art, which were covered in some places with moss that afforded an agreeable relief to the eye. Through apertures in the roof light was admitted sufficient to enable us to discern our way, which we continued forty or fifty feet, until we came to a narrow portal that opened into a hall much larger than the one we had quitted. Following my conductor within I found myself in the presence of a young female of exquisite form. She was sitting at a table covered with a cloth of gold and purple, in which was wrought some of the principal events of history. Her attention was deeply fixed on a ponderous volume, that lay before her written in Oriental characters. A gorgeous lamp of fretted gold threw its pale light upon her face, and discovered a set of features singularly beautiful. Her complexion was pale, and her countenance wore a soft and languid air approaching to melancholy. Her dark tresses thrown back upon her shoulders, displayed a high, arched forehead, as if destined in an eminent degree to be the "proud empire of thought." Struck with the beauty of the fair mortal before me, I gazed upon her with wonder and admiration, without noticing any thing around me, until the old man, advancing towards her, said, "Daughter, the stranger before thee would behold the Phœnix and the grand festival."

She raised her head, as if for the first time conscious of our presence, displaying a pair of mild blue eyes of the softest expression I ever beheld, and pointing to a dark curtain that covered the eastern part of the cavern bid me behold what I desired. The curtain began slowly to upfurl, the lamp emitted a paler light and the grotto itself appeared as if undergoing a change. Emotions of fear began to steal over me, and I turned to look for my conductor, but he was gone. The curtain was entirely upfurled, the grotto appeared to have fled away, and I found myself with the mysterious female by my side standing on an elevated summit at the banks of the reedy Nile. Far as the eye could reach o'er the dark waters, myriads of light galleys were glancing, each of which was illuminated with a profusion of lights that made the waves appear a sea of glowing flame. The sound of the tabret and cymbal, mellowed by the softer notes of the flute and other instruments of Oriental music, the shouting of the votaries, and the lively chants of the priests increasing in loudness as they approached the shore, announced the grand quincentesimal sacrifice.

Having landed upon the shore, they entered upon the grand and imposing procession. Before went the priests with solemn step attired in their long

H*

hieroglyphical habits; then came the different sacred animals of the Egyptians all fantastically adorned, among which I observed the Crocodile curiously ornamented with shells, rings and chains of gold. Next followed choirs of maidens attired in shining robes, bounding gracefully along to the sound of the music, while countless myriads of votaries and strangers, bearing offerings of gold and frankincense and myrrh, closed up the long procession. As they continued on I observed, at a distance, through the obscurity of night, a huge pile, which I concluded was the august temple. The dark shades of night had begun now to soften into the sober gray of morning twilight, after which the rays of the rising God diffused rosy tints over the eastern sky, that soon deepened into the richest crimson and gold.

They played the majestic air usual on such occasions and prepared to enter the temple. The Sun in godlike grandeur now flashed upon the gilded colonnades of the temple, when all thrice bowed reverently to the deity, (the last time falling upon their faces) and then entered within.

To attempt describing the gorgeousness of the scene would be vain; the following, however, will serve to give a faint idea of it. The interior of the walls was of the finest Thasian marble, with its beautiful veins heightened and polished until they resembled pictures of the most delicate finish. The floors were tessellated with marble squares of different kinds and colors united together by gold, and disposed and contrasted so as to have the most striking and beautiful appearance. In one corner of the temple stood the lavers for the priests to wash in before and after sacrifcing. They were of the purest ivory, inlaid with gold, and variegated around the brim with studdings of carbuncle and topaz, and other most precious stones. These lavers were supplied with water, that gushed like sparkling silver through pipes of richly fretted gold, terminating in the head of Sphinxes. Among the massy colonnades of curiously wrought marble, that supported the frescoed ceiling, were disposed, in endless variety, statues of the different sacred animals, and small golden pillars, the tops of which were inlaid with gems in such a manner as exactly to form the different sacred flowers; every color and tint being accurately represented by gems of similar hue. In the centre, upon a throne of polished gold, irradiated with emerald and carbuncle flashing like fire, crowned with a diadem that resembled rays, was a grand representation of the God himself, so placed as to receive the full light of the sun. Circled around his radiant throne, like pages to attend his commands, stood the light-winged Hours. Without this circle was formed another circle, of months, that, grouped in companies of three each, formed four minor circles, including the four Seasons—rosy-coloured Spring with her mantle of light green and her garland of flowers, Summer with her crown of golden wheat, Autumn purple as to his buskins with the juice of trodden grapes, and hoary Winter with his glassy eye and snowy beard.

As I gazed on the beauty of the splendid scene, there suddenly reigned universal silence through the temple. Not a sound was heard, save the light footsteps of the priests and their attendants as they prepared for the most august rite of the ceremonies. Presently the smoke of the incense arose until the temple was darkened; the music burst forth

in one peal of astounding sweetness, and shouts of
"the Phœnix," "the Phœnix," were heard in deafening acclamations, until the confusion of voices
and music resembled the rushing of mighty waters
mingled with the awful sound of raging winds.—
On came the Phœnix soaring through the air, seem-
ingly without exertion, (for its broad pinions were
spread out motionless upon the breeze,) and sailing
in royal majesty along, it approached the temple,
bearing, on its broad back, the excavated mass of
myrrh in which it had deposited the embalmed body of the parent bird.   At the vestibule it alighted,
furled up its broad pinions of gold and crimson and
placed, on the threshold, the sacred burden it had
borne; and then spreading its beauteous wings on
the breeze, sailed again through the light air towards its spicy country.   I continued gazing with
admiration on the airy volant, until it was nearly
lost in the distance, then turning to look upon the
priests who were about closing the ceremonies, I
found the temple fading on the view, and receding
from the sight, until as it became hardly distin-
guishable in the distance, the dark curtain began to
fall, and shortly universal gloom reigned through

the grotto. The mysterious female was gone, but in
returning again from the cave the light of the moon
poured through clefts in the rock that formed the
ceiling, and on looking up I read, "Grotto of Imagination," the letters of which were formed by light
breaking through the openings of the rock.   Then
did I know, that the Genius, who presides over ruins,
had transported me to the cave of Imagination.

TO MY WIFE.

BY JOHN COLEMAN.

———

We've loved through good and ill report,
 Alternate gloom and shine;
Midst every effort to divert,
 My heart was always thine:
And now it well repays for years
Of doubts, of agony, and tears,
 To know that thou art mine,—
To see thee standing by my side,
My lovely, young, and blushing bride!

Before the altar we have stood,
 Our lips have breathed the vow,
To cleave through evil and through good,
 And ever love as now.
Our hearts, our hands, our fortunes, one,
I press the lips at last mine own,
 And gazing on thy brow,

I feel my throbbing bosom beat
Tumultuously wild and sweet.——

'Tis sweet to think no more we part,
   Till death dissolves the tie,
That heart shall ever cling to heart,
   Beneath Love's happy sky.
Thy hand in mine, 'mid rapture's glow,
I fear not sorrow's tear shall flow,
   If thou, my love, art nigh;
Thy presence shall forever be
The light of love and bliss to me.——

O dearest! check that trembling sigh,
   Forbid that rising tear;
Let smiles but sparkle in thine eye,
   What hast thou now to fear?
My pride and happiness 'twill be,
Through life to love and cherish thee,
   Most gentle and most dear:——
Believe me, thou shalt ever find
My heart unchanging, true, and kind.——

MY BIRTH PLACE.

BY EUGENE.

There is a spot on this green earth,
  I think of with delight;
'Tis that dear spot, which gave me birth,
  Where first I saw the light;
That place, where in my childhood's hours
  I pluck'd life's gayest, sweetest flowers,
    Which strew'd along my way,
    In rich profusion lay;
      And, saw on high
      A clear bright sky,
    In mildest azure drest,
      Which ever smil'd,
      And me beguil'd
    In happiness to rest.

There's many a scene, round that dear spot,
  On which I love to rest,

    I

Scenes that can never be forgot,
   But ever in this breast
Wake strong emotions of delight,
   Whene'er by memory's fondest light,
I view that happy home,
   From which I'm doom'd to roam;
        And think how sweet,
        'Twould be to greet
    That lovely place once more;
       And by the wood,
       And river flood,
   To wander as before.

I've wandered 'mid rich roseate bowers,
   And breath'd the sweetened air;
But never found as fragrant flowers
   As grew and blossom'd there;
Nor lilies e'er as fair have seen,
As modest deck'd that hallow'd green;
     And never more shall meet,
    With flowers again as sweet,
       As when the gale
       In that dear vale,
    Would steal their scent away;
     Around were spread,

On earth's soft bed,
Dress'd up in colours gay.

O how I loved, abroad to roam,
  While in my childhood's hours,
Around my mountain-cinctured home,
  And pluck the sweetest flowers;
And hear the lark's full matin song,
Which floated on the air along,
    While perching on some spray,
    Or sporting o'er the lay,
        Or through the shade
        Of opening glade,
      Darting along in glee,
        The merry birds,
        In tuneful words,
      Join'd in wild revelry.

And where the silvery fountain gush'd,
  And its clear streamlet poured;
And where the foaming waters rush'd;
  And where the torrent roar'd;
And where the wildwood hid the stream,
From sparkling in the sun's bright beam,

I'd wander free from care,
With bosom light as air;
Or in the brook,
With baited hook,
The fish unwary take,
Or in a boat,
Fearless afloat,
I'd paddle o'er the lake.

'Twill pensive feelings o'er me fling,
To think of that dear spot,
And sadness to this bosom bring,
When pondering o'er my lot;
Thus doom'd in anxious doubt to stray,
From that dear spot I love away.
Oh! how I'd love to be
Where the sad willow tree,
Would mournful wave
O'er the still grave
Its drooping branches slow,
Where laid at rest,
On earth's cold breast,
One slept in silence low.

'Twould be delight again to pour
  My heart's full feelings forth;
And weep in silent anguish o'er
  That sacred spot of earth;
Where now another's laid his head
To slumber with the wakeless dead;
    Snatched off in childhood's bloom,
    And "hurried to the tomb."
      To the full heart,
      It would impart,
    A sweet consoling balm;
      That "joy of grief,"
      Would bring relief,
    And every struggle calm.

I*

LINES TO A LADY AT PARTING.

BY EDRED.

They tell me lady that thou goest
   Abroad to grace a foreign land;
Well,—be it so,—no tear of mine
   Can stay thy footstep on our strand.
'Tis useless, too, to heave a sigh—
   For dreams of past but happy hours,—
They flit—like spirits round the dead,
   Or perfume over withering flowers!

Ah! when the humblest dwells beneath
   The voiceless, gloomy ground,
Some friend, at even tide, oft heaves
   A sigh to swell his funeral sound;
So, maiden, when on other shore,
   My dirge's music strikes thine ear,
Oh! may I ask that angel eye
   To grant the tribute of a tear!

OCEAN.

BY T. S. ARTHUR.

O THOU unfathomable deep!
  Whose mountain chainless waves,
Untiring o'er thy bosom sweep;
  Or murmur in thy caves!
In thy dark chambers many a gem
  More bright than e'er hath shone
In beauty's glittering diadem,
  Lies buried and alone!

But ocean, 'tis not on thy breast
  Alone commotion's waves
Are felt, nor worth unknown at rest
  Within thy secret caves;
There's many a billow of distress,
  Which o'er the heart will roll;
And many a surge of woe will press
  Upon the drooping soul.

And many a glittering star would rise,
    Triumphantly on high;
And shed a lustre o'er the skies
    Of science, but they sigh
Alone, and waste their souls pure fire,
    (By penury weigh'd down)
Obscur'd by clouds, which damp desire—
    Neglected, and unknown.

Oft when the sun with rosy charms
    Encircled round is seen,
Just rising from thy humid arms,
    Clad in his richest sheen;
Thy swelling breast hath gently curl'd
    Beneath the breeze that blew,
And Phœbus o'er thy watery world,
    His dazzling splendour threw.

But e'er again he'd sunk to rest,
    Thy billows roll'd on high:
And wild commotion siezed thy breast,
    And clouds hung o'er the sky;
And the gay ship, which rode in pride
    Upon thy waves at morn,

Is whelm'd beneath the foaming tide,
  By raging tempests torn.

'Tis thus life's morning oft will spread,
  All lovely o'er the sky,
And hope a sparkling brightness shed,
  Joy sweetly smile on high.
But oh! how soon clouds gather o'er!
  And hopes bright star glows dark,
And floods of deep affliction pour
  Upon life's fragile bark.

LOWEKA.

BY J. N. McJILTON.

THE sun had sunk in his pride, behind the hills
of the west, and was buried beneath the deep blue
wave of the ocean; the soft tints of the twilight
had faded—the thin clouds of the night had gathered—the pale moon burst from between them and
rested in silence upon the hill. Whokahonti and
his chiefs had chosen the place for their repose,
the fires of war blazed around them, and their
victim was bound to the stake. The groans of the
stranger rose from the midst of them, and mingled
with the wind of the wilderness. Whokahonti
rolled his dark eyes in fury,—he thirsted for the
blood of the son of the white man, but scorned to
wreak his vengeance while the shadows of the
night were upon the earth. The warriors rested
upon their spears, still smoking with the red blood
of their enemy. Impatient they waited for the
sun of the morning to chase the dews of the night
away, and tinge the early cloud with his light.—

Then should the spirit of the son of the stranger, leave the place of his sorrow, and join the ghosts of his fathers in the land of the shades.

Loweka was the daughter of Whokahonti; she was the pride of his age, and beautiful among the children of the forest. The snows of sixteen winters had melted from the earth, since the one that gave her to her mother's arms. She moved upon the plain in the pride of her beauty, and joined with her friends in the chase. Her jetty tresses swept the ground as she passed, and her eye flashed with the fire of youth. She eyed the stranger with affection, the flame of love burnt in her bosom, and she longed for the mists of the midnight,— for she said in her heart "the stranger shall be free."

The moon was in the centre of the heavens, the shadows were straight upon the earth; Loweka wrapped herself in her white mantle and thrice walked round the sleeping chiefs of her nation.— A cloud swept across the pale face of the moon; she approached the white stranger; in an instant he was free. "Fly," said Loweka, "for the footstep of revenge is at thy heel." A warrior chief raised his head in the silence, he saw the white robe of Loweka pass swiftly before him; he thought the spirit of the night had descended to guard her sleeping warriors, and again he sunk to slumber in the stillness of the forest.   The mists of the night were dispersed, the first gray tints of morning spread upon the sky.   The chiefs awoke, and the hatchet of death thirsted for the blood of its victim.   They looked for the stranger —he was gone.   The features of Whokahonti grew dark as a stormy cloud, the hatchet of his fathers cleft the air, and he swore, by the demon of the tempest, that it should yet riot in the blood of the white man—that an hundred scalps should tremble upon his spear, ere his deadly wrath should be appeased.

The warriors closed round their chief.   His soul gathered blackness as he spoke:—"guile," said he, "was upon the white man's lips, and deceit lay loose upon his tongue; he approached us with the pipe of peace and gave us the hand of friendship; we offered him the calumet and he smoked it in our midst.   The Indian was kind and spread the feast before him; the flesh of the buffalo was roasted upon the embers; the fruit of our land was laid plenteously in his presence, and the rich corn of the valley smiled at his approach:—such has been the deeds of the Indians to the sons of the stranger, but black has been his ingratitude. He saw thee in the fullness of thy enjoyment, and in the pride of thy youth; he aimed at thy ruin, for his thoughts were intent upon thy downfall; and like the panther of the wilderness, he has sought his victim to his home. Such is the faith of white men. The misty wave of the ocean, is red with the Indians blood, and the sand upon the shore has been crimsoned with the life-wave of the savage.— How has the tall oak of the forest been plucked up by the roots; how has its branches withered, and been scattered to the wind. Sons of the forest! still you may have hope—for you are yet mighty in your strength—you may yet rejoice, for the great spirit of the waters is with you; the dying curse of our fathers rests upon his head, and vengeance shall be upon the land of the oppressor; let your petitions to the great spirit, rest upon the mighty, and terrible to the white man shall be the Indian's arm; you shall be to him as a whirlwind

K

and as a storm, and his pathway shall be scattered with desolation and with death. Whokahonti and his warriors shall yet rejoice in the fullness of revenge."

The voice of the warrior chief died away in the desert, but dear to the soul of the Indian were the words of his lips; a hundred voices rose upon the air, and a loud vengeance was pronounced upon the white man's head. The warriors separated, the desert and the forest were hunted in the pursuit of the stranger. They returned in silence, for disappointment sat heavy upon them; again their voices loudly roared through the forest, and again they swore eternal enmity to the race of the pale faces.

Two moons had passed, Loweka and the stranger were still wandering amid the wilderness and through the desert. Loweka had told her love to the white stranger; he listened with delight to her artless tale, and soon his bosom burned a mutual flame. She had often besought him to reveal to her his name, for "thou art dearer to me" said she, "than life, nay thou art dearer than revenge to the soul of the savage; for thy smile I'd cross the

trackless desert, and dare the fury of the tempest
for thy love. Then conceal not thy name from me,
for my heart is united to thine forever." The
dreams of the white man's early youth rose up before him; he thought of the days of his youthful
love, and the briny tear gathered in his eye, for
grief lay heavy at his heart. The companions of
his early days, the home of his childhood, his
dear, native land, each thrilled through his
soul, and brought the gushing torrent from his eyes.
"O why art thou sad," returned the child of the
forest, "and why are thine eyes filled with tears?—
art thou fearful of Loweka's love, or do the dangers of the desert distress thee? tell me thy sufferings and thy name, for thou hast filled me with sorrow." "My name," said he, "is Zadib, of the race
of the white men; beyond the green isles of the
ocean dwells my father in a stately mansion. My
sisters have gone to the land of the blest, where
the spirits of the just rejoice." "Then dry thy
tears and hush thy sorrows, for Loweka will be
thy sister; she will wipe from thy forehead the
cold dews of the night; she will watch thy sleep-

ing hours, and protect thee from the jaws of the panther."

The third moon had commenced, the shades of evening fell, the gathering storm roared fearfully in the distance, the howls of the wolf were heard, and the buffaloe fled swiftly before the rising tempest. The heavy thunder rolled deeply through the clouds, and the forked lightning streamed across the stormy bosom of nature; the great spirit walked amid his clouds, and commanded the bursting torrent to fall upon the earth. Loweka had been taught to brave the dangers of the tempest, and she walked fearless amid the warring of the elements. Again the fierce lightning flashed—the eyes of Zadib became dim—he fell—the rock entered his side—and the warm blood flowed. The darkness of night now fell heavily upon the earth; the lightnings of heaven fiercely blazed amid the darkness. Loweka saw the crimson tide from Zadib's breast, and though she walked undaunted amidst the thunder's roar and the lightning's blaze, the sight of his blood struck terror to her soul, and fainting she fell at his feet. Zadib's wound was but slight; he caught the trembling Loweka in his arms and entered the forest. Exhausted he laid his burden at the foot of a sturdy oak. The lightning scathed it, and it fell tremendous at his feet—his hope was ended—he threw himself upon the ground and invoked the spirit of the storm to cease his rage. A moment the wind is hushed—he hears amid the darkness, the barkings of the hermit's dog, hope springs again in his breast, a light glimmers through the trees—a moment more and the hermit of the hill is by his side.

Loweka was borne to his cave, and laid upon his bed of straw. Zadib watched the bright beam of innocence, that glowed in her features, and besought the great spirit to bend from his temple in the clouds and restore her to his love; he sought again the forest to give vent to his sufferings.— The lips of Loweka quivered—her eyes opened,— she saw the aged hermit bending over her fair form; "friend of the great spirit," said she, "tell me, was it Zadib's blood that stained my cheek? tell me where he lies, and if the cold hand of death is upon him? I'll seek his printed footstep on the sand, and at night when the dim ghost of the dead are wandering near me, I'll point them to

K*

the hallowed spot, and tell them the story of my sufferings. I'll seek his grave, and in the silence of the desert will protect it from the coming tempest. O cruel spirit of the deep waters, why was I left alone to wander the earth in silence? Shade of my mother look from thy land of spirits and guide Loweka's wandering footsteps." Zadib entered the cave, she screamed with joy, and restored was Loweka's fainting soul.

The morning rose fresh upon the earth, the sun drove the clouds from before him, and shown in splendour upon the mountains. They joined in the chase—Loweka bounded the plain like the deer of the forest, alone she climbed the rough sides of the mountain, and sought the wild haunts of the deer: she had learned the use of the bow—the hart fled before her in vain, and she hunted the buffaloe to his glen.—Nine moons had silently stolen over them and the tenth had commenced her course; Loweka's bosom was full of sighs, for sorrow had gathered like a thick cloud in her breast. On the wings of the blast she poured forth her sad song in secret, and mingled her sighs with the wind of the desert. Zadib wiped the salt tear from her eye, for his manly breast heaved with the anguish of his heart, and his bursting soul gave vent to the rushing shower.— "Why," said he, "Loweka dost thou mourn, and wherefore does the darkness of thy soul arise?— Thou shalt not wander alone by the dark stream of the desert, nor shall thy steps by the side of the mountain be taken in grief."

"O Zadib! within my bosom there is a voice, that tells of the years that have rolled away. It comes from the land of the dim ghosts of my fathers, and I am tossed like a beam upon the wave of the troubled ocean."

"Then Loweka cease thy weeping, the hermit of the hill shall bind us together, the great spirit shall bless our union, and the cloud of other years shall pass away." The evening came, the watery moon rose high, and the hermit returned not,—fatigued with the chase, he had sunk exhausted and was slumbering by the stream of the mountain. Zadib left the cave and sought the hermit in the desert, and upon the hill; the sun arose above the mist of the ocean, before he found the place where he lay. They returned to the cave. Loweka was stretched

upon the hermit's bed of straw.   Zadib approached her,—the paleness of death was upon her cheek,
—she raised her head,—"Zadib" said she "my spirit soon shall pass the land of shades; my mother's
ghost is waiting to receive me and rejoices in the
firmness of Loweka.   Upon the wing of the night my
spirit shall often wander by the mist of the stream,
it shall mix with the wind of the mountain, fearless it shall brave the desert's storm and like a dim
flame, it shall bound the darkness of the midnight.
Zadib, my father was the white man's friend—he
delighted in peace, and his heart was full of joy,
when he could do aught of kindness to the stranger;
he rescued him from the panther, took him to his
home, spread the fruits of the chace before him, and
at night sung him to rest.

"The white man was ungrateful,—and before my
voice was heard upon the earth, his spear was red
with my brother's blood,—when I was born my
mother showed me in her arms to the great spirit;
she told him I should be his, if he would grant them
revenge upon the head of their foes.   My father's
voice rose high in vengeance; when I grew up he
bade me swear by the curse of spirits to be the

white man's enemy. He pointed me to the bright
sun and bade me imprecate his wrath upon my
head whenever I should be kind to the foes of the
Indian. I have drank the juice of the poppy and
feel its effects in my bosom; my mother's spirit
smiles upon me, and will welcome me to the airy
dwelling of the dead; before me is a land of everlasting love, soon will I bound by never failing
streams, where the voice of music is heard, and the
hand of oppression shall be felt no more." Her voice
was hush'd in death, and her spirit's airy form
passed swiftly to the shades of rest. Such was Loweka's fate. The hermit consigned her to the tomb,
and Zadib wept by her side. "I will protect" said
he "the hallowed spot that covers her mortal dust,
and if the hunter's heedless tread should be upon it,
more furious than the tigress of her whelps bereft,
I'll tear the base intruder; the rose and lily shall
spring upon the sod, that wraps her dear remains;
the chaste bird of night shall warble forth its melancholy strain upon the boughs that wave o'er her,
and her spirit shall glide o'er the turf like the thin
vapour upon the bosom of the unruffled waters. O
why was I left alone to sigh my love to the bosom

of the wind, that only mocks me with the echo of
my voice!   Soon, Loweka! my fleeting spirit, tired
of its prison-house, shall join thy wandering shade.
Two moons and Zadib was laid low by the side of
Loweka.   The hermit alone was left to tell, the
weary pilgrim as he passed, the story of the lovers.

THE EAGLE'S DEATH.

A SKETCH.——BY EDRED.

Where wintry winds sweep o'er the faded leaf,
And rock the mighty giants of the grove
That gem the mountain's front like Emeralds—
The pale-brow'd Eagle sleeps—

      *   *   *   *   *

Hark! the wild war-cry booming on the air,
Palling fair nature like the Siroc's breath
That crumbles Eastern fanes! Hark! hark! again!—
And lo—behold the fiery flaunting flag
Lifting its folds far o'er the advancing clans:—
Like swift-wing'd tropic bird of crimson plume
Flying to bathe—deep in the sunlit wave;
Or some huge shatter'd sphere of living flame—
Rushing to quench its burnings in the sea—
Lo—it advances! Behold the exulting bands
Glittering with mail of proof and spears
That erst did teach the proud to tremble!

Hear—hear the rolling drum,—the trumpet's note,—
The cannon's earth quake voice—tell tale of wars:—
And seé—the Eagle wakes as by his cliff
The conflict sweeps with tempest tread.

        ——————Behold his balanced wings,
And the dark eye fierce—flinging back the film
That curtained it in quietness of sleep,
A beaming eye bright as those silvery orbs
Mirror'd in beauty on the trembling sea!
He seems the god of battles whilst he looks
With scorn and vengeance on the deeds of death!
See how he thrusts aside the yielding air
And hovers o'er the children he hath loved,
To be their guardian spirit in the fight.
Ha! why droops his wing, why shuts his lofty eye?
The noble bird that often proudly dared
To dip its bosom in the blazing sun;
Or, like another Joshua, drag it back
To cheer his chosen warriors with his beams—
Falls mid the strife!—Death nestles in his heart,
And breathes its venom through his faltering wings.

A FRAGMENT.

BY ORAN.

In all the nameless charms of youth and grace,
She grew to womanhood; her loveliness
Reflecting all the smiles of maiden beauty.
Oh! it was sweet to gaze upon a sight so fair:
She seem'd like some pure spirit, sent awhile
To shew the dwellers on this barren earth
How glorious their future home, and then
Return to her own native clime.——
As glided through the crowd her sylph-like form,
Her features lighted by a smile serene,
That spoke of peace and happiness within,
With health and beauty sparkling on her cheek,——
No marvel knees should bow, and hearts confess,
They ne'er had seen such loveliness before.——
       *   *   *   *   *   *

He loved her—fondly lov'd her; who could not?
Yet never dreamed his passion was return'd;

L

It was enough for him to gaze upon her charms,
And in his secret thoughts, by day and night,
Imagine how supremely blest the man
Who ever could possess a gem so rare.
'Twas ecstacy to know he breath'd the air
And trod the same beloved ground with her.
If in the mazes of the circling dance,
Her hand to his, by *simple chance*, was press'd,
What thrilling glow it sent through all his veins!
'Twas like electric touch, and penetrated to
The heart's remotest avenue!—
Yet still distrust and fear seal'd up his lips;
He never spoke of love; and though
The ravages it made upon his peace were deep,
He fail'd not, day by day, to drink
Still deeper of the poison so delicious.——

　　　*　　　*　　　*　　　*　　　*　　　*

And did *she* never know or feel the secret
Witchery of love?   Was *her* heart ne'er moved
And into gentle agitations thrown?
Did *she* ne'er ask what 'twas had robb'd her of
　　repose?
And waken'd sighs so new within her breast?
Ah yes! the tell-tale blush, the downcast eye,

The stolen glance, whene'er his manly form ap-
    peared,—

The thousand little artifices maidens know so well,—

These all, in love's own silent language, spoke.—

Yet was *he* last to know she lov'd;

He could not think that joys so exquisite were his.

But as, by small degrees, the happy truth

Reveal'd itself, with bright and rapturous ray,

Oh! what a flood of bliss it pour'd upon his soul!

    *   *   *   *   *   *

TO —— ——

BY ELLEN.

———

WHERE the raging billows sweep,
Thou art in thy quiet sleep,
Resting thy unconscious head,
With the cold and silent dead.

O'er thee no funereal note,
With its deep ton'd dirge doth float;—
But the requiem o'er thy grave,
Is the murmuring of the wave.

No white marble walls enclose
Thy fair corpse in calm repose;
But the ocean wave enshrines,
And the sea weed round thee twines.

Over thee no flowret blows,
But around thee coral grows;
And its stony leaves are prest,
Hard against thy gentle breast.

Stealing through the ocean wave,
If some sun-beam greets thy grave,
Coldly will the straying ray,
Fall upon thy colder clay.

It may light awhile the gloom
That hangs darkly o'er thy tomb;
And the sparkling gems may gleam,
Welcome to the wandering beam.

But thou heedest not the glow,
That is greeting thee below;
Or that plays around thy head,
Lighting up thy lonely bed.

Rest on in thy quiet sleep,
'Neath the overwhelming deep!
There's a peace and calm for thee
Even in the restless sea!

L*

TO MARY.

Methinks to-night thy sparkling eye,
  A brighter rapture wears;
It seems envelop'd in a sigh,
  Yet melts not into tears.

What is the charm that there doth burn?
  My dearest Mary, say;
It seems a diamond in an urn
  Of liquid, sparkling day.

'Tis not a tear that revels there,
  Diffus'd the orbit o'er—
No, that would dim the thrilling star,
  That gives it all its pow'r.

'Tis love itself in Mary's eye
  Dissolv'd in liquid bliss;
I feel his charm in Mary's sigh,
  And drink him in her kiss.

                                        T. L.

THE MANIAC

BY ...

In the spring of 18.. I... ...

...that calm, secluded happiness of ... ...
so grateful to those ... ...
oppressed by the fatigue ... ...
transactions. I accordingly resolved ... purchase ...
a small country residence, where blessed with

THE MANIAC SHEPHERDESS.

BY ROBERT MACHIN.

"Around her rose and myrtle lay
And laurel, amaranth and bay;
And while the flowery wreath she wove,
She sung her plaintive lay of love."

SCOTT.

In the spring of 1817, I returned to my native country impaired in health, and in the decline of life, after a residence of twenty years in the interior of India. Having amassed wealth sufficient to render further employment of any kind unnecessary, I determined to devote the evening of my days to that calm, secluded happiness of rural retirement, so grateful to those laboring under infirmity and oppressed by the fatigues of unremitted mercantile transactions. I accordingly resolved on purchasing a pleasant country residence, where blessed with

the society of a beloved mother and two affectionate sisters, I might pass a life of contentment and
ease, aloof from the bustle and turmoil of life; and
did not wait long until I observed that a farm was
offered for sale at the distance of about twenty
miles, which, from the description, I judged to be
just such an one as would suit me.   I resolved on
visiting it immediately and, while doing so, availed
myself of the opportunity of calling on an early
friend, who lived about five miles from the above-
mentioned place.   After a social evening spent in
such hilarity as might be expected from friends so
long separated, we parted for the night with the
intention of visiting the estate together on the following morning.

It was a fine morning and every thing in nature
seemed buoyant with life and joy; and after pausing
a hundred times to express our admiration of the
scenery, we, at length, came to the confines of the
aforesaid estate.   It was situated along the side of
Loch Lomond and embraced some of the most
grand and romantic scenery of the much admired
country around the Loch.   Its long winding vales
covered with luxuriant herbage, its clear streams,

its high craggy cliffs with the airy summits of the Grampian hills towering above the clouds at the western environs, could not fail to impress the mind of the beholder with sensations of thrilling delight.

Alighting from the carriage we resolved to take a short ramble, and passing down a winding valley, espied a young shepherdess reclining under a broad oak, busily occupied in wreathing chaplets of willow and wild flowers, that decorated in rich profusion all around the green velveting of the sward. On the right was a grove of tall elms and cedars, interspersed with thick matted underwood blooming with vernal blossoms and loading the air with fragrance. At the bottom rolled a murmuring creek which, flowing a short distance, formed itself into a beautiful broad lake, that reflected on its smooth surface the sloping mountain. On the left was a level piece of ground entirely clear of trees, that extended as far as the lake, where it ended in a craggy precipice hanging perpendicularly over the water at the height of about forty feet. Having glanced at the surprising beauty of the place our eyes turned again upon the young Shepherdess. She was intently engaged upon her wreath and did not perceive us. Around her was a large flock of beautiful sheep, some browzing on the herbage, others frisking about on the sward, while others, like their mistress, reclined under the shade of different trees. Gazing on the beauty of the being before me it appeared to me as if Pales had again visited the earth, in all the beauty and graces of melancholy loveliness. Her long golden tresses unrestrained by comb or fillet, wantoned in the light breeze, displaying as they fell back upon her fine shoulders a forehead, high, fair and beautifully formed. Her light hazel eyes had a peculiar expression that well accorded with the pallid melancholy of her features: and though her dress was extremely plain there was something in her appearance, that bespoke uncommon dignity of person. She presently burst forth into a plaintive air, with a pathos inexpressibly painful, for it seemed as if the chords of her soul were wrought up to an intensity of feeling, even to bursting; her eyes assumed a wildness, and her features such an air of vacancy, as convinced us that the unfortunate maiden laboured under aberration of intellect. Looking upon the stream she discovered our shadows, started from her seat, and bounded down the glen with the speed of an Antelope.

"What an adventure" exclaimed I, "surely friend Marlow, you have heard of this interesting creature before and can inform me something respecting her."

"I will inform you of her melancholy history," said he, and he gave me the following relation:—
"She is the daughter of Sir Robert Norman, whose proud and arrogant behavior towards his inferiors, you, no doubt, recollect when we were boys together. This haughtiness increased as he advanced in years and affluence, until he came to look upon his inferiors as an order of beings far beneath him, as the worm, that crawleth upon the turf: but alas! he has passed to that silent region, where all is equality; where the king and the beggar slumber together, a solemn warning to all that "pride goeth before destruction and a haughty spirit before a fall." Sir Robert and his family which consisted of his wife and daughter, the unfortunate shepherdess whom you have just seen, and a maiden sister, were accustomed to spend the summer months at

Nairnbræ, where they enjoyed, in the parties given
to the surrounding gentry, the pleasures of the metropolis, without suffering its sultry confinement.—
Though of haughty and austere manners, Sir Robert's heart was full of tenderness and love towards
his amiable wife and daughter, which increased as
the graces of the one softened into the dignified
charms of age; and the beauties of the other bloom-
ed in all the loveliness of womanhood.   The striking beauty of Lavinia's person was such as could
not fail to produce pleasing emotions in the breast
of any father however callous: but in addition to
the pleasure the personal appearance of his child
excited in the breast of Sir Robert, the unassumed
dignity of her manners, the sweetness of her disposition, and the high order of her intellect, expanded
by diligent study far beyond the circle that circum-
scribed the mind of most of her sex, flattered highly the natural pride of his heart, and drew forth his
highest admiration and most sincere love.   It was
during the summer residence at Nairnbræ, that Sir
Robert sustained the loss of his amiable consort.—
She was seized with a violent fever, that terminat-
ed her existence in a few days and was buried in

the family cemetry of Nairnbræ. During her ill-
ness the grief of her husband and daughter was violent, but when hope became utterly extinct and
the amiable wife and mother was about to be
forever removed from those to whom love had so
tenderly united her, their sorrow was inconsolable,
and many a twilight, after her body had been committed to the dust, their tears copious as when they
first flowed at her decease, fell upon the green turf
that covered her remains. The spirit of the haughty man was humbled before the Lord; affliction
bowed down his lofty heart and the tears of sorrow
melted the frozen sympathies of his nature; so that
to those around him, his domestics, his tenants and
dependents, his actions were divested of his former
hauteur and unfeeling insolence, and characterized
by kindness and humanity.

This salutary change, which affliction had wrought,
continued until leaving Nairnbræ, he again mixed
with those of proud, aristocratical feelings like
himself, and in a great measure had obliterated
the good impressions which the death of his inestimable wife had made. Nearly a year had now
passed and the sultry season commencing, Sir Ro-

M

bert and his daughter set out for his country residence. It was a pleasant day in June and nature smiled in joyous beauty. The azure arch of Heaven was beautifully flecked with light clouds of purple and crimson and gold. The meadows extended far and wide clothed in verdant green; and fields of grain, with a gentle breeze, waved like the agitated billows of the deep, while every mountain and grove and glen was radiant with beauty and vocal with melody. In order to enjoy the breeze and the beauties that presented themselves on their way, it was determined that Sir Robert and his daughter should ride in his open landau. Towards evening they approached near his residence, when the driver, by a violent concussion of the vehicle, was thrown from his seat with his head against a rock. The horses instantly took fright and set off at full speed; when the father, endeavoring to seize the reins, was precipitated senseless from the carriage by the boughs of a tree under which the horses passed. Lavinia seeing no hope of escape swooned away. The horses continued their flight, plunging from ledge to ledge down the side of a steep hill, until making a sudden turn they were

about to rush down a precipice, where the carriage
and lady it contained, would have been dashed to
pieces, when a young shepherd seeing a female in
such imminent danger, jeopardizing his own life,
rushed before the furious horses, and as they were
just about making the desperate plunge, seized the
reins with a grasp that the circumstances rendered
gigantic, and having curbed them and confined them
to the boughs of a tree, hastened to the relief of the
female.   What was his surprise and commiseration
when he recognized in her, the lovely daughter of
that woman, who ,had taken him an orphan from
poverty and wretchedness; and having given him a
tolerably good education, placed him in comfortable
circumstances.

He took her in his arms and with a fleet step
glided down the glen, and sprinkling her face with
the cold waters of the lake, with much joy, soon
observed symptoms of returning animation.   After
several deep drawn sighs, she opened her soft expressive eyes and started back, while crimson blushes
suffused her cheeks, and inquiring the particulars
of her rescue, expressed unbounded gratitude for
the magnanimous exertions, he had made to rescue

her from imminent death. The father, who had received but little hurt, except the stunning of the blow and the fall, was instantly sought and assisted to gain their house, which stood at a short distance, while proper care was taken of the driver, whose head was dangerously contused by the fall. The young shepherd's interposition between danger and his daughter, elicited Sir Robert's admiration and gratitude, but excited in the tender breast of Lavinia that glowing interest, which manly beauty, magnanimity and disinterested devotion never fail to awaken in the grateful breast of woman.

Thankfulness for the preservation of his child overcame his prouder feelings, and Sir Robert gave Allan Burke a hearty invitation to dine with him on the following day, which was accordingly accepted. Lavinia in the evening determined upon visiting her mother's grave, and as her father, from the fall he received, was unable to accompany her, she went alone. It was the impressive hour of twilight, when the sombre objects around, the faint twinkling of the stars, and universal stillness dispose the mind to serious and contemplative reflection; and the feelings of Lavinia were softened

down into a calm and holy awe, as she approached
the grave of her departed mother, until she felt, as
if, she were treading upon the portal of the eternal
world. When she arrived at the cemetry, she observed, amid the branches of the weeping willows,
that surrounded the grave, a person in the attitude
of prayer, and presently in the tender aspirations of
the suppliant, recognized the voice of her deliverer.
To see the virtuous youth pouring forth his noctur-
nal orisons at the grave of her, to whose benevolence, he owed the religious sentiments which he
had imbibed, and the comfortable station he held,
touched the feelings of Lavinia more than his
intrepid interposition between herself and death,
and her heart melted into sympathy with him in beholding his affectionate and grateful recollection of
the dead.

The shepherd arising from his knees espied a
witness of his unobtrusive devotion, glided hastily
away through the bending branches and was soon
lost in the adjacent grove. After indulging the tender sorrow, that filial affection would necessarily
feel in such sacred and solemn circumstances, Lavinia returned to her father and retired to repose.

M*

The following day Allan dined with Sir Robert, and Lavinia was struck with admiration in finding his manners, though he had been of lowly birth, to be perfectly genteel and more captivating from their unstudied elegance, than the cold, formal precision of those termed *well-bred*. Sir Robert himself was brought to admire the virtues and modest graces of the rustic lad, and informed Allan, that if propriety directed his conduct, he would soon reward his kind and manly services, with an office much more honorable than the one which he held at present; to which the shepherd modestly replied, that, what he had done or ever could do, would be but a small return for the kindness which he had already received at *his* hands, and at the hands of his most inestimable wife. After dinner the shepherd returned to his flock, having made a favorable impression on the heart of Sir Robert and entirely engaged the affections of his daughter.

Lavinia's heart had been a stranger to the soft emotions of love, and when it became prepossessed in favor of one so noble, so virtuous, so beautiful and deserving, it glowed with all the fervour and devotedness of woman's first affection.—

Every prospect, that erst was beautiful, was now dull and pleasureless; save the one which embraced her beauteous shepherd and his snowy flock. Every sound of music was harsh and monotonous save the mellow breathings of his dulcet pipe. And every company was cheerless, for amidst its sickening brilliance figured not her beloved Allan. Business called Sir Robert to the metropolis for a few weeks, during which time proposals were made to him for his daughter by a gentleman, who to great personal accomplishments, added the highest intellectual attainments, and from his wealth and noble standing in society, was such an one as he would wish to have as a son-in-law.—As the father knew that Lavinia appreciated his character highly, and had received, with evident pleasure, frequent marks of his particular attention, he did not hesitate, to inform the gentleman that it would be highly agreeable to him and that he doubted not that it would prove equally agreeable to his daughter, and accordingly was the bearer of a letter from the gentleman to Lavinia.

When Lavinia had proceeded a short space, her pale countenance and the starting tear, convinced her father, that its contents were not of as pleasing a nature as he had anticipated. Her countenance, became more overcast as she continued reading and when she had finished, her eyes, as if dreading the scrutinizing gaze of her father, fell upon the floor, and she continued wrapt up in melancholy thought. Her father broke the long silence by chiding her delay in expressing her sentiments respecting the offer of the noble suitor; but was answered only by her tears. On being urged to speak, she begged her father to be contented for her to remain unmarried observing that though the gentleman, who had done her the honour of proposing for her hand was in all respects worthy, she felt no prepossession in his favour, and that she could not think of bestowing her hand upon one on whom her affections were not placed. Finding her obstinate in her determination, after remonstrating with her on the futility of her objections, her father in violent anger left her, irritated at his wishes being thus thwarted, especially, after the assurance which he had given her suitor of his success.

The true cause of her disinclination he suspected, and resolved, in the vengeful humor of his soul, upon a punishment of the most fiend-like kind. During the day his countenance wore the dark scowl of determined vengeance, every word he uttered was full of impressive terror and awe, and every gesture exhibited the high wrought excitement of his wrathful soul. After tea he appeared more calm, threw himself upon a couch, and presently appeared to be dissolved in sleep. Seizing the opportunity, Lavinia withdrew from the apartment and hastened to the young shepherd to make him acquainted with the events of the day. The notes of his flute filled the grove with melody and diffused a melancholy joy over the heart of Lavinia as she glided along to join her lover. He was seated under a large oak near the precipice, where he had rescued from destruction the female, whose kind love had since evinced the sincere gratitude she felt for the deed. Around him was scattered the fleecy flock, which he tended, browsing upon the dewy grass. The bright beams of the moon were dancing upon the ruffled surface of the blue lake, or glancing in silver beauty through the thick boughs of the waving trees. The blue arch of Heaven was resplendent with its starry garniture; the stream rolled along in murmuring me-

lody, and every prospect was calculated to awaken
pleasing sentiments; but Lavinia was insensible to
the beauties, that before were wont to diffuse pleasure o'er her heart; her words were few and faint;
her countenance was pale, and the soft lustre of her
bright eyes was dimmed. "What ails thee Lavinia," said Allan. "Art thou sick?"

"My heart is sick," replied the maiden and leaned
her head upon the bosom of her lover. "I will tell
thee all presently; but Allan, where is the nightingale, whose melody from yonder bough has been
accustomed to thrill our bosoms." As she spoke a
lonely dove perched itself upon the deserted bough
of the nightingale, and filled the grove with its
plaintive, piteous cooings. " 'Tis a bad omen I
fear" continued Lavinia, "which I feel strengthen-
ed by the dismal forebodings and dark presentiments of my own breast."

"Why distress yourself with superstitious fears
my love; surely you will not let the cooing of a pi-
geon cast a gloom over your happiness."

"Nay, my fears and sorrows are not imaginary
Allan; a gentleman, with the approbation of my father, has sued for my hand; I have rejected the of-

fer, informing him, that at present I feel no desire to change my situation, for how could I bear to be separated from thee, my love! my deliverer! and be given to another."

"And has your father acquiesced in your wish?"

"He has not. He received my objections, with indignation; his eyes flashed with anger, and his countenance became dark and terrible as death.— His rage I fear not on my own account, but, oh! Allan, should he discover our love what will be the effect of his passion towards thee." "Death!" responded the loud voice of her infuriated father, as he rushed forward from the oak under which they were sitting and run his sword through the heart of the shepherd. Allan endeavored to arise, but the weight of Lavinia, who having clasped her arms around his neck, had swooned away, prevented him, and he fell backward upon the ground, and fixing his eyes steadfastly on the countenance of his murderer, shortly after expired. The murderous man was rivetted to the spot; the dying gaze of the murdered shepherd, like the head of Medusa, rendered him a petrified statue, that was unable to move.— His vengeance now was sated, but oh! how the

thorns of conscience rankled in his bosom. The
generous youth, whose intrepidity had saved the
life of his darling child, lay at his feet murdered by *his* hand, and even within sight of the precipice where the noble and intrepid deed was done.
Recovering from the first shock which the infernal
deed had caused, without stopping to raise his
child from the body of her lover, he hastened to
the house, and despatched several servants to have
them conveyed from the place they then were. Lavinia was brought to with the utmost difficulty; but
the sun of reason had set to enlighten the horizon
of her mind no more. She was a maniac. Nothing
could restrain her from the flock which her murdered Allan had tended; and her father after several fruitless attempts to restore her to reason, permitted her to remain with it, as she appeared to be
satisfied and tranquil only when with it. The ac-
cusations of his guilty conscience, the ruin which
he had brought upon his lovely daughter, and the
hatred which he believed every one entertained
towards him, preyed upon his spirits, undermined
his health, and brought down his hoary, sinful head
with sorrow to the grave." "Beneath this oak" con-

tinued my friend, advancing towards the tree under which the maiden had been seated, "the unfortunate shepherd suffered, and here is his grave decorated with the chaplets of his maniac love."

Leaving this place with which so melancholy a story was connected, we continued our way to the mansion and made known the object of our coming. The person's terms who had the disposal of the property being fair, I immediately became the possessor of Nairnbræ, among whose fountains, groves and lawns I enjoyed more pleasure and uninterrupted good health, than had been my lot for several years. The shepherdess and her flock as an appendage of the estate still remained with us, and nothing ever gave me a more melancholy pleasure, than to observe the proofs of this faithful creature's constancy and affection, continued amid the entire alienation of intellect. One morning while taking my usual ramble, on nearing the oak where she reposed at night, I heard the loud bleating of lambkins, and approaching nearer, found them surrounding the body of their mistress, from whose hand they were accustomed to receive the morning salt and meal. She lay with her arms around the grassy

N

grave, her head lying partly on the grave and partly resting upon her shoulder, as if she was in a deep
sleep.   I took her by the hand.   It was cold and
clammy.   Death was upon her brow and the spirit
of the lovely, innocent and unfortuate shepherdess
had flown to its Creator.

JUAN.

A SKETCH.

———

Lady, farewell! I breathe no sigh—
  No mark of care, is on my brow,—
No tear betrays, to stranger's eye,
  The pangs, that rend my bosom now,—
I do not mourn, that time has swept
  My brightest dream of life away—
I cannot weep as men have wept,
  O'er hopes betray'd, or love's decay!

Young JUAN paused; while o'er his pallid brow,
The flush of high excitement passed—what
The cause, he dar'd not, to himself, avow;
It was not hope—alas! he could not blot
From memory's page, if all else were forgot,
When first unto his startled vision, fate
Reveal'd the coming gloom of his dark lot—
Then sank his heart, beneath th' oppressive weight;
And as all joyless *this* he feared no *future* state.

And yet the keen observer, gazing there,
To scan the various passions of his soul,
Would seek in vain, the calmness of despair,
That potent spell, to whose dark, stern control,
Man's wildest passions, as they onward roll,
Are chill'd, and perish—as the flow'rs that raise
Their stems amid the tempests of the Pole—
His eye told not this—no! its kindling blaze
Betray'd a spirit, which would joy to gaze,

Upon the ruins of his broken heart;
And smile, to see the visions of his youth,
In all their freshness, at a word, depart
Stripp'd of their beauty, by the hand of truth!
Hath the world aught of pow'r, such minds to
    soothe?
The drop which blackens in a heart of pride—
Shedding the poison of a serpent's tooth
On all around—nerving the soul, to bide
This wreck—yet wear the mask of joy, to all beside.

E'en so it was with him—how sad the change
The briefest hour of misery brings
On all who comes within its gloomy range!
Past, now, were all the gay imaginings,

Which gave the hues of Heaven to earthly things—
Alas! the joys that fancy pictures to the mind,
Glide like the moments urged by rapture's wings—
Still lives there one, who does not hope to find
In those bright dreams, the bliss denied to all mankind.

A dreamer he had been—from childhoods hour,
A creature of enthusiasm—not one
Who lov'd to seek some lone, sequester'd bow'r
And, far from social converse, dwell upon
The memory, of what the past had thrown
Upon his view.—Then he had not redeem'd,
Were his the pow'r, one moment which had flown;
He lov'd the cheerful world, because he deem'd
Its buoyant creatures, pure and happy, as they seem'd!

And yet, at times, he loved to steal apart,
And hold communion with himself—and pour
Th' impetuous feelings of his swelling heart
Forth to the stars, and bid his spirit soar
Freely along,—their beauties to explore—
For hours—'till his imagination pin'd
And droop'd beneath the burthen which it bore—
And *then*—the breathing of the very wind,
In such a mood, were fraught with music to his mind.

N*

At length he lov'd—oh there's a world of bliss
In love's first throbbings, in the youthful breast!
A joy, as pure, as centres in the kiss,
The mother breathes upon her child at rest—
A joy, though often felt, yet ne'er éxprest;
To *him*, it was a glimpse of paradise,
Which gave to all his hopes a purer zest—
He knew not then, how soon that vision flies,
Leaving the broken heart to mourn its obsequies.

He lov'd—The star of his idolatry
Beamed in a form of fair, unrivall'd grace;
A form just budding from the witchery
Of earliest youth—and hast'ning to its place,
Among the riper idols of our race—
The age of joyous feelings—when the mind
Starts into new existence—there to trace
Through years of disappointment—still to find
The phantom joy—a mock'ry fleeting as the wind.

She was not beautiful, the maid he lov'd,
But oh! there was a magic in her smile,
He ne'er had met before—yet he had rov'd
'Mong fairest forms, whose coldest look would wile

A Seraph from his course—though every isle
Of starry light, shone brightly on his way—
It was the breathing of a heart—where guile
Had never enter'd, gentlest wishes lay,
Like shaded flowrets, shunning the warm glance of
    day.

She was a pale and gentle creature, save
When the excitement of her feelings threw
A passing blush upon her cheek; and gave
To her transparent brow, the roseate hue
Of warmest fancies, bursting into view—
And then the flashings of her soft blue eye,
Were rays of intellect, fresh dawning through
The windows of her soul—most radiantly
A glance will tell, where latent gems of genius lie.

And who, however dull his own may be,
Loves not the gushings of a gifted mind;
Nor feels one hallow'd thrill of extacy,
Like the first sight of Heaven to the blind:
Who long for that one look of bliss, have pined,
When list'ning to the fervid thoughts that steal,
Sad'ned with fragrance, as a summer's wind,

From female lips—when aided by the zeal
Of chast'ned eloquence, which they alone reveal.

Her soul was fraught with pure and holy things;
A nursery of glorious thoughts,—which dwell,
Alone with those, where wildest romance flings
Her gay deceptive witch'ries—Few can tell
The sweet bewild'ring poison of that spell,
Which steals upon us, in the morn of life,
Hiding its treasures, in the heart's lone cell,
Where fancy, sick'ned of the world's dark strife,
Retires, and paints, an ideal world, with beauty rife.

Juan lov'd her—There is a love, which years
Of sin and suffering can never tame!—
Amid ambition's after hopes and fears—
The lust of wealth—the pomp of pow'r; that flame,
Like Zoroaster's God, glows still the same!
    Still 'mid the gush of tears, by manhood shed
For friends estrang'd—hopes wither'd—wreck
    of fame—
E'en on the couch of death—that hour of dread!
This passion lingers, when all else of earth has fled.

He lov'd her, and was lov'd—but soon a blight
Cross'd his fond cherish'd hopes, and he became

A weary traveller, bereft of light,
And left, to grope his way, on life's dark plain,
A reckless being, void of end or aim.
Enough that they were sever'd—parted too,
By one, who 'neath the mask of friendship's name,
Conceal'd his treacherous purpose, from their
    view—
The tale is old—to man, what tale of guilt is new?

I said he lov'd—and when he found his love
Was hopeless—he wept not—he could not tame
His haughty spirit down to weep—but strove
To hide his anguish, and subdue the flame,
He knew that sympathy was but a name,
For that base feeling of the heart, which finds
A joy in gazing on another's pain
The first, last, weak resource of feeble minds,
His spirit, scorn'd the frail communion, which it
    binds!

Time, months and years roll'd on, and still, he bore
Her image deeply shrin'd within his heart—
A poison, rankling to its very core;
And yet, he could not wish it to depart,
He now had wiser grown—had learn'd the art,

Of hiding all his feelings—and to seem,
So aptly did he counterfeit his part,
The soul of whim, and pleasure—little deem
The idle world, the pangs he bore, untold—unseen!

C. J. L.

YOUTH AND AGE.

BY ALVARA.

O where are they now, the lov'd ones of youth?
Once fondly united in friendship and truth,
Affection's bright mantle was thrown round our
      hearts,
We felt her sweet influence—the bliss she im-
      parts.

O 'twas life's sunny time, her sky was serene,
Her cold blighting winters had ne'er yet been
      seen,
Passion's stream murmured gently—its cascades
      not loud,—
They fell in the sun-light that scatter'd the
      cloud.

Human life is uncertain, the aged would say,
Her smooth gentle current may change in a day,
Adversity's tempest will often arise,
And clouds of affliction hang dark o'er the skies.

The voice of experience we heard without fear,
Though gentle the warning, unkind 'twould ap-
        pear,
Life's current was smooth, and it pictured the sky,
As it hung its blue curtains unspotted on high.

We held the delusion secure to our hearts,
O! blissful delusion! what joy it imparts!
But it burst like a bubble—reality came—
Life's dream is uncertain and " friendship a
        name."

O where are they now? the loved ones of youth!
No longer united in friendship and truth,
No longer in rapture we meet round the hearth,
And hush'd is the voice of our innocent mirth.

O some have departed across the blue wave,
And some slumber silently in the cold grave,
Some alone, and forgotten, in poverty mourn,
Despis'd and forsaken, neglected, forlorn.

But oh! some are chang'd, there's no longer the
        smile
That will gladden the bosom and sorrow beguile,

That sweet smile of friendship which lightens the
heart,
When we meet they are careless, and cold when
we part,

This touches the heart, those who erst were so
kind,
So lov'd, and so loving, thus alter'd to find;
But life's spring time is ended, its bright skies are
fled,
And the flowers that grew thick o'er its pathway
are dead.

o

THE CRUCIFIXION.

The morning sun,
In splendor bright,
Gilt Salem's tow'rs
With living light;
And streak'd the fair etherial blue
With tints of gold and purple hue;
Earth bloom'd in loveliness and grace,
And rob'd in smiles was Nature's face;
But soon the fading sun grows pale,
Quench'd are his beams o'er tower & vale.

The quaking earth
Is sunder rent—
The rocky hills
The battlement—
The bursting tombs
Disclose their dead;
The saints forsake
Their earthly bed;
And midnight gloom
Veils earth & skies,
For, "Lo! the God
Of nature dies."

1

THE RETURN.

BY GEORGE GORDON.

———

Invidious grave! how dost thou rend in sunder
Whom love has knit, and sympathy made one.

BLAIR.

———

THE transaction of some business in Europe in
which my father had a concern requiring a personal attention, I was selected by him to superintend
it, and was accordingly obliged to forego the pleasures of domestic bliss, the endearments of a large
circle of youthful companions, and the still more
tender and cordial joys of sympathetic love.

The object of my affections was one, in whom
was concentrated all that could dignify the female
mind and person, and her soul was a hallowed temple, in which every virtue and excellence had a
shrine. Though only of the age of fourteen, her
hand, morn and evening, amongst the necessitous,

dispensed blessings, that make glad the sunken eye
of poverty, and cheered the gloomy countenance of
despair; and her lips distilled streams of comfort,
that refreshed the burning fever of penitent guilt,
and allayed the pangs of a wounded conscience.——
Her consolations and bounties, like the rains of
Heaven, which are sent upon "the evil and the good"
were dispensed alike upon the worthy and unworthy sufferer.　All the needy were subjects of her
anxiety, her kindness and her care.　From our
most tender years, the sweetness of her disposition,
the interesting softness of her countenance, and
the goodness of her heart, had won my admiration;
and as she verged towards womanhood, her beauty
and virtues becoming more developed daily, I felt
an increasing regard and tenderness for her, until
she became the grand centre around which all my
thoughts and affections revolved.

I had poured forth the effusions of my heart,
and she had received them, not with the shock
which disgustful affectation appears to feel, but with
the simplicity and native modesty of artless innocence.　She favored my suit, reciprocated my
love; and we had for some months past enjoyed all

the happiness arising from hearts fraught with overflowing sympathy and love. This happiness alas! was now to be interrupted, for a wide sea was to roll its broad expanse between us. Our hearts were sorrowful, but anticipation, amid our tears at parting, pointed to a speedy return; when our hearts and hands were to be united to part no more. This was some stay to our minds, and with many embraces and vows of remembrance I tore myself from my love, my family and friends, and proceeded to Philadelphia, whence we were to sail. At the expiration of four years, during which time I had seldom heard from home, I had finished my business and was ready to return.

With feelings to be imagined only by those who have resided a long time abroad, I embarked for my native country, and after a long and wearisome passage, I found myself at Philadelphia and took stage for the residence of my father, which was in one of the little villages in the interior of Pennsylvania. Towards evening I arrived within a mile of the village, when, after giving orders respecting the disposition of my baggage, I alighted, resolving to indulge in the pleasure of passing on

o*

foot through the scenes among which in youth I
had spent some of the happiest parts of my life.——
A soft, and somewhat mournful feeling passed over
me, as I continued along, finding something at every step to call up youthful recollections. Desolation was upon the plain, and autumn's gray and
sombre mantle was thrown o'er field and forest.——
As I passed along the grove, the discolored leaves,
twirling roughly through the branches and strew-
ing the plain, whispered to my ear the lovely and
the blooming fade and die; and the thought came
o'er me, how changed, how lowly may be many,
whom I left blooming in health and beauty. The
sun, as a small part of his course remained, gleam-
ed faintly in the western sky, and the idea crossed
my mind, that the bright hopes I entertained might
like him be sinking into rayless night.

After sometime I gained the summit of a little
mountain from which I had a view of my native
village. The smoke curled gracefully from the
chimnies of the milk white cottages, around which
were neat palings of white and green. There
stood the moss covered church half enveloped
among yew and cypress, and there the village

school with its little dome and vane; but its long
level inclosure was not covered over with the
noisy groups that were accustomed to gambol upon
its green. Scarcely a person was to be seen in
the streets. All was still and silent. As I stood
the solemn toll of the village bell fell slow and
mournful upon my ear, and presently the rich, sad
melody of the organ, and the voices of those in the
funeral chant, floated mournfully along on the
breeze. I stood as if bound to the spot by a spell,
until I saw the sable bier issuing from the church
preceeded by the musicians, and attended by a
train which constituted the entire inhabitants.—
The procession moved slowly along, while the low
notes of the funeral hymn gave a deeper solemnity
to the scene. I made towards the graveyard with
a hasty step, anxious to see the last ceremonies
that were about to be paid to some acquaintance,
bound to me perhaps by friendship or consanguini-
ty. Presentiments that became darker as I approached the graveyard, harassed my mind. It
might be an intimate friend—my sister—my father
—my mother. I felt an unusual quickness of
breathing. My pulse was weak and fluttering.—

As I came up, the usual rites were ended; the grave was filled up, and the final dirge was sounding an eternal farewell. I joined the train and inquired of a person who stood near me, who the person interred was. "The loveliest flower of the village," replied he; and a gathering tear showed that his heart felt what his lips uttered. I admired his noble soul, but felt grieved that I had not received a direct reply. "The name," said I.— "Cordélia Hepburn." My soul sickened. Darkness spread over my eyes. Strength—sensation— failed me, and I sunk to the earth. When consciousness returned, the mother of my being was watching over me, and the countenance of my sister, smiling through tears, met my beloved gaze.— But after the transports of my recognition, the fearful truth, that the fondest hopes of my heart were blasted, came o'er me with its dread reality, and my bosom felt even amidst the love of a mother and a sister, that it was lone and desolate.— The lovely Cordelia's frame was too fragile to endure our long separation; she pined away, and consumption had consigned her to the tomb.

Since that time I have been a lonely pilgrim upon earth; for my thoughts are above the skies where I expect a reunion with her spotless spirit. I repine not at God's dispensations; for I receive with calmness, prosperity and adversity alike.— Hopes on earth I have none, and therefore cannot be disappointed. And as it respects desires I have none, with the exception of one; which is that when death shall have laid his cold hand upon my brow, I may be laid beneath the willow that waves above the grave of Cordelia, while the same solemn, touching, and sublime music shall waft on its tones my wearied soul to heaven.

MARIA VERMELLI,

TAKING THE VEIL.

BY EUGENIA D'AVALON.

I saw her on the verge of womanhood—
Like the young morn, she bloom'd in rosy grace,
And threw a chaste and soften'd light around
On all who met the sweetness of her smiles.
Her eyes were soft and tender as the dove's—
Her step was light and graceful like the roe,
And her bland voice fell gently on the ear,
Like the sweet sounds of pipe or Eastern lute,
O'er some lone lake by distance mellowed.
The light of her young mind like Hesper's ray,
Gleam'd with a brilliance, glorious, soft and bright;
And her young breast was fill'd with feelings pure,
And overflowing as the gentle dew,
That trembles in the petals of the rose.
Her light and loveliness around her drew

MARIA VERMELLI.

Lith. of Endicott & Swett.

A train of warm admirers, eager each to gain
A treasure so divinely fair and rich.
Among the youths that worshipp'd at her shrine,
Was Giumar of noble race descended;
Possess'd of youth and beauty, skill'd in wiles
Of lure and love, he stole upon her heart
By sighs of feign'd affection, and by looks
Of soft and melancholy languishment,
Until her bosom heav'd responsively
To the feign'd feeling of his treacherous soul;
When with a heart of adamant, he spoil'd
Her of her virgin beauties, and consign'd
To winds and wintry storms, the fairest flow'r
That blush'd in beauty in green Uva's vale.
The ball and sprightly dance, where once she shone
The gayest, fairest of the happy train,
She join'd no more. Amid the silent grove
And by the rills, where once with Giumar,
Rapture with rosy wings led on the hours,
O'er hopes decay'd, o'er strong affection's ties
Sunder'd she mourn'd, and weeping brooded o'er
The utter desolation of her heart.
To fit her erring soul for Heav'n she sought
The calm seclusion of the convent's walls.

* * * * * * *

The day arriv'd, and habited in white,
Maria came with slow and solemn step
To bid a last farewell to worldly scenes,
And earth renounce to fix her thoughts on Heav'n.
Her face was pale, her brilliant eyes were dimm'd,
Yet a soft, pensive melancholy threw
A sweetness o'er her features, that she look'd
As sadly fair as angels, when they bend
In heavenly sorrow o'er the dying couch
Of suffering Innocence.——The Abbess comés,
And as Maria kneels before the cross
Her eye illfated met Giumar's gaze.
One long loud shriek, burst from her frenzied lips,
Unutterable woe was on her features trac'd;
Then came the settled calmness of despair,
With'ring th' excited energies of life.
She bow'd her knees and breath'd her vestal vow,
And with it breath'd her spotless soul to Heav'n.
By Uva's walls Maria lowly sleeps,
And by her side her penitent Giumar.

THE LAST ROSE OF SUMMER.

BY CLAUDIUS.

See Flora, here still secret lies,
And breathes around, her perfum'd sighs,
      Upon the dying year;
Pale autumn, with his arid blast,
Did ne'er such incense round him cast
      As lingers sweetly here.

A rose, I'm sure, her bosom wears,
From which, her zephyr fragrance bears,
      Upon his fading wing;
I kiss the perfume of the flow'r,
Which should have hung on summer's bow'r,
      Or deck'd the lap of spring.

Ah! lovely rose, I see thee now,
And feel the transport of the bough,
      Which bears thy blushing bloom
But vain thy smiles, and vain thy sighs,
Pale death resistless o'er the flies,
      And blasts thy sweet perfume.

    P

Thus beauty in unguarded hour,
Is doom'd by fate's insatiate pow'r,
      Like the sweet flow'r to lie;
Unconscious of a danger nigh,
She trusts to man, her bosom's sigh,
      And droops in misery.

PASSION.

Holding its wayward course along,
  Deep hidden in the breast,
A viewless flood of passion swells,
  Its foaming billowy crest.

Sweeping along untam'd by thought
  Uncheck'd by reason's sway,
It holds its steady course along,
  Its deeply tide worn way.

Swelling its banks if e'er 'tis check'd,
  And proudly dashing o'er,
A raging cataract, that deep
  Its foaming waters pour,

Or boiling in its fury there,
  With strong resistless force,

PASSION.

It bursts away, and dashes on
   Its wild unheeding course.

Or calmly rising like the storm
   In silent majesty,
Rolling its fleecy, clouds along,
   The melancholy sky.

And swelling its deep chainless flood,
While waves on waves still roll
   Along, till bursting in its might,
   It overwhelms the soul.

O what a calm then settles in
   The breast that's torn and riven,
But 'tis not that sweet placid peace
   Which from above is given.

'Tis like that calm, when from the sky
   The furious storm is roll'd
And nature pauses in her course
   Her ruin to behold.

Passion still holds its steady way
   But silent in its course,
Till pent again it bursts away
   With overwhelming force.

THE SIMOOM.

BY N. C. BROOKS.

The sound of trumpet, clash of zel
Upon the fluctuant ether swell;
While to this clangor soon succeeds
The heavy tread of warriors' steeds,
And lo! above the horsemens' plumes
The towering flag of Almach comes:
A phalanx of a thousand lances
Amid the glowing sunbeams glances,
While in the flaunting banner's rear
Are thousands arm'd with bow and spear.

Their joyous shouts, that echo far
To the thick groves of Ebular,
And ring along the cliffy side,
Of far resounding Elbro's tide,
The mournful, sad and sorrowing wail
Of female woe, that loads the gale;

THE SIMOOM.

The long and beauteous, weeping trains
Of maidens drawn along in chains,
And murderous Almach's smiling eye
Of plunder tell and victory.

Why moves the banner on no more?
Why stops the clanging trumpet's roar?
Why are the spears upreared to heaven,
Into the sand in terror driven?
Why stands the victor band and why
Quails cruel Almach's fiery eye?
Lo the Simoom! its deadly cloud
Rolls darkly towards the warrior crowd,
The gloomy messenger of Heaven,
For fate and mortal vengeance given.

The furious charger's echoing tread
Is ceased as by instinctive dread,
His fiery courage grows more tame,
And his broad nostrils breathe no flame;
When slow and solemn, onward driven
He sees the vengeful cloud of Heaven.
Dismay is on the warrior band,
They suppliant fall upon the sand,

r*

And deprecate the awful wrath
Of Heaven about to swoop their path.

But onward came the dreadful blast
And breath'd destruction as it pass'd.
The heaven-spurn'd suppliants meet their doom,
And make amid the sands their tomb.
The steed, that champ'd the bits in pride,
Sinks lifeless by his master's side;
The broad dry desert of Ashere's
Bestrew'd with falchions, bows and spears,
And the lone flag waves high in air
Above the mouldering corses there.

THE CHINESE BRIDE.

BY BRANTZ MAYER.

"Talk of oblivion! when by cares opprest,
This heart shall cease its throbbings in the tomb,
Then may I lose remembrance of his doom,
And meet him in the regions of the blest."

MILLHOUSE.

THERE is a wild promontory on the coast of China, not far south of Macao (the only christian settlement on those shores) in connexion with which is told the following tale:—

Not far from this spot lived, some few years since, Léung, a Mandarin of high and vast resources, who in his youth, had passed with the utmost credit through all the departments in the schools of Pekin. So great, indeed, were his talents that he soon received the notice of Government, and was rewarded with a post of high honor and trust. He married early; but unlike the generality of Mandarins, never took a second wife: the only offspring of this marriage was a daughter, who forms the subject of this story.

Amoë was still of tender years, and possessed in a superior degree all those amiable qualities, which render woman the sweetest companion of man in his moments of enjoyment, and his only blessing in times of sorrow and misfortune, when she was wedded to the son of a wealthy Mandarin. Atchung her husband, in whom all the manly virtues were blended, was in the navy of his country, subject to every immediate call upon his professional services, and forced to endure all the vicissitudes of wind and battle. It was about the time of his nuptials with Amoë, that the southern coast of China, and the islands lying between the coast and the Phillipine group, were infested with Latrones, collected from the scum of the Indian population, and perhaps some European countries, who, driven by penury to despair, sought to relieve their wants by preying on the vessels of Europe and the East.— Their depredations were committed chiefly upon vessels of the smaller kind, and to so great an extent, that it at length became evident to the Chinese powers, that they could no longer remain silent, but must interfere authoritatively by arms.

Atchung was despatched in this desperate service, before a month had passed over his connubial happiness. It wrung the tender heart of Amoé to think that there was to be so speedy a termination to the gay hopes she had forseen of a long and uninterrupted enjoyment of his society. Her heart was of a peculiarly susceptible mould, and had chosen hope as its only food. Already in her young life, she had often experienced the sad disappointment of her dreams and whispered to herself, in secret musing that, hopes are like the children of our early years, and the greatest misery of human life is to be called from weeping over the grave of one, to drop our tears upon the tomb of another.

At times she dwelt with fear upon the deadly warfare, among desperadoes and outlaws, in which he was shortly to be engaged; and then she used all the blandishments her love could invent, to lure him from battle; but the voice of honor called him, and all the sighs and charms of his wife could not silence its imperative tones.

The parting moment came at length. Her eye was clouded like a sky that bodes no good to the traveller. A spirit of prophetick despondency seemed to have conjured up in her mind, evil anticipations for the expedition; but her grief was voiceless, it appeared only in the deep, feeling expression of her jetty eye. She bent her tall figure against the bosom of her husband, and the tear of his manly sorrow fell upon her cheek.

She watched from the promontory, whither she had been carried in her sedan chair, Atchung's barque disappearing upon the dim horizon as it was wafted towards the Isles where, perhaps, he was to endure many a storm and contest before she should again press him to her heart.

She tried to hush her sorrow, but the light notes of the guitars of her maidens, or their sprightly voices, as they mingled together in chanting the melodies of her country,—the balmy air as it came, winged with a thousand perfumes of the flowers, that stood on her verandah, or the tempting sight of the richest fruits could not still the pain of that unexpected separation. She truly felt the full tide of feeling, which is always to be found in a youthful and enthusiastic heart as yet uncontaminated by the foul contact of the world, and that shadowy feeling clung to her like the dark clouds, which cluster about a mountain's brow, destroying its verdant beauties by their beating and continual showers.

The allotted time for the cruise passed, and Atchung did not return; but the fame of his victories reached Amoé's ears, and the pride woman takes in the glory and exaltation of her husband, served to alleviate for a time his prolonged absence. She was told, too, that he had undertaken another expedition, the command of which had been entrusted to him, on account of the prowess and skill he exhibited in his former combats. So quickly, however, was this armament equipped at a distant port, that he had not time to steal a look at his beloved wife, before he was summoned to his station.

Whilst this second expedition was preparing, the pirates supposed, and justly too, that the efforts of government against them were merely relaxed and not entirely ended; that, in fact, it had only paused in order that it might gain additional nerve for future contests. Under this impression, they improved the recess, and making a common cause, concentrated their strength.

The yellow, imperial flag of China floating from the masts of Atchung's four war-junks—no longer excited fear in the pirates' breasts, or forced them to seek security in concealment or flight. As soon as they heard through their spies, of the arrival of another naval force among the Isles, it was determined upon a hasty council, to engage the foes as speedily as possible, with a force sufficient to keep them in play until wearied by loss of men, or length of engagement, and then to pounce upon them with a host of vessels which should, during the precarious part of the contest, be secreted among the deep bays immediately bordering the scene of action.

The four Chinese junks arrived, after a short passage, within sight of the Latrones' decoy vessel, and immediately chased it until they came up with four more of the enemy becalmed between two small, thickly covered islands. Atchung instantly made signal for battle. The gongs were beaten— the soldiers threw on their arms with the rapidity of thought—grasped their strong spears and stood firmly behind their thickly woven shields;—in a moment the decks wore the semblance of warlike display and discipline.

The battle commenced.—Cannons roared from both pirate and Chinese, and died away in echoes among the hills. The beams of the vessels were soon marked by the trickling blood of those, who so lately strode proudly over the deck, and whose bosoms glowed with the high hope of extermination. The pirates fought bravely, until though much weakened, they had made a great impression on the strength of the Chinese. It was at the moment when the brave Atchung was pressing with his wonted intrepidity a slight advantage he had gained over his adversaries, that the smooth bosom of the sea, which seemed almost locked between the two islands, appeared covered with the enemies' vessels, rowing swiftly from every nook in the shores, every deep bay and wooded inlet.

The force of the marauders was far superior to that of China; Atchung saw his impotency, but he knew that a retreat in his shattered condition would be useless. His only hope was *despair!*

The contest became close, until pirates were mingled with Chinese, and they fought hand to

Q

hand;—clouds of the darkest smoke blackened the atmosphere over this scene of murder. The fate of the day was soon decided.—Three of the Chinese junks yielded, their crews either slain or made prisoners; but Atchung's vessel was still a scene of strife, and a mark at which all the combatants aimed; if her commander yielded, a most cruel murder would be the certain consequence, he, therefore, resolved to dispute his life to the last, and fall as a brave warrior loves to fall.

He saw, that a stream of fire was issuing from the bows of his vessel, and rapidly consuming her; the thought that her final explosion would bury numbers of his country's enemies with him, inspirited him to fight—gashed and bloody as he was. But this last hope was denied. The enemy observing their danger drew off, and left the vessel to her certain fate. Finding no more foes to contend with, Atchung resigned himself calmly to his lot, endeavoring to persuade his comrades from seeking safety by swimming to the enemies, but could not prevail,—they left him to a man, and left him amid the solitude of the burning ruins of his gallant vessel. At last the awful moment came—the powder caught—a dreadful crash followed—a dark volume of smoke went up to the sky, and the noble barque floated no longer. Her timbers were scattered far over the sea and the brave commander, who had so often led her into battle and retired a conqueror, perished in her ruins.

Such was the melancholy story, that but a few months after her marriage, was told in the dwelling of Amoê. Her friends saw the despondency to which she was a prey, and kept the dismal tidings from her ear. She observed the time for her husband's destined arrival approach—arrive—pass—still he was not with her. She asked for information about him, but she was answered only by the tearful eye of her parent, and a smothered sigh, which but too plainly betrayed the sorrow it sought to conceal. Naturally possessed of a fanciful mind she formed to herself a thousand ills, which might have befallen him, and, again, fancying a bright picture, hoped for happy hours. The memory of earlier days, too, shed a momentary glow amid her gloom like a brilliant star that throws a faint ray over the darkest skies. Time seemed to linger on a leaden wing—yet Atchung came not.

It was, at last, thought advisable by her friends to disclose his death, supposing, that, after the first burst of sorrow her grief would be sobered, and that time would render her resigned to so early and severe a dispensation.

The tale was told. Neither friends nor flowers possessed any longer a charm to raise her drooping spirit, or place once more a smile upon her lip.— She would sit whole days in moody silence; and when it was broken by approaching strangers, she would motion them away. Still there were moments when she would listen to music, but it was of a melancholy cast and told of broken hopes and sorrows of a similar and as deep a dye as those, which had been meted to her with no sparing hand. The light of her days seemed to be extinguished—the music to whose measure her heart responded was stilled forever. When temporary disease paled her brow, she *felt* that there were no longer the smiling lip and anxious eye that hovered around her feverish couch in other days. The arms that once were thrown in the solicitude of love about her, no longer pressed her to a bosom, that beat for her alone. And she heard no more those thousand little enquiries, which fall so pleasantly on a fond wife's ear. Instead of the communications that used to engage their evenings, she drew from her bosom his picture, which he had sent her before marriage, and often while seated in her solitary chamber, many an eloquent tear dimmed its brilliancy.

This uninterrupted seclusion, and unceasing thought upon *self* induced delirium. Her home could no longer contain her. She wandered to the promontory overlooking the sea, whence she had seen Atchung's sail blending like a dim star with the clouds on the horizon. There would she set and rave to the winds—and converse in her delirious imagination with the dead. Her visits to this spot became more frequent and longer, until finally, she took up her abode entirely in a small hut, built on the farthest verge of the cliff, which had been the habitation of fishermen. Her only companion was a dog, the present of a foreigner to her husband in Canton.

All the efforts of her friends to withdraw her from this dreary abode, were unavailing, and to force they could not resort; however, the greatest
Q*

care was taken to render her abode comfortable
and to provide all the necessaries and luxuries of
life, whilst she persisted in enjoying the melancholy delight of dwelling like a sea bird over the
stormy ocean. Thus she lived for many months,
wearing out daily in strength and appearance,
whilst an almost demoniac wildness settled on her
features.

＊　　　＊　　　＊　　　＊　　　＊

It was a dark and tempestuous night,—the very
spirit of the storm seemed to be moving in its re-
velries,—when the heart-broken woman was aroused from her feverish sleep by the loud beating of
the waves upon the rocks at the foot of the promontory, and the rolling of the thunder as it pealed in deep murmurs over the sea. She started
from her bed, and rushed forth amid the storm,—
she stood upon the brink of the precipice, whilst
the spray dashed over her as it skimmed from the
jet black waves beneath. She called loudly upon
the name of her husband and it was echoed among
the hills whilst the storm paused to gather strength
for its lightning and more dismal tones for its thunder. The raging sea and its dark canopy of clouds,
a mong which the thunders were rumbling, beheld

by the continual flashes, presented too gloomy a
picture for even a sane mind to regard with composure. But Amoé seemed not to heed it. She
bent over the rocks, and listening to the echoes of
her ravings construed them into replies from her
dead lord. She fancied that he called her—and
screaming—"I come—I come,"—sprung forward
as if to clasp an aërial figure. With her hair
streaming and whistling in the blast, her face pale,
worn and haggard,—and her eyes glaring with all
the wildness of a maniac—she fell over the precipice!—a shriek and a hard dash on the rocks below, told the end of her brief, but unhappy career.

The storm subsided before the dawn; morning
found the sea once more smoothed into tranquility,
and the sunbeams sleeping in their golden quietness
on its bosom. Amoé's attendants brought her food
as usual; the hut was tenantless; they searched the
cliffs in vain, but glancing over the farthest point
of the promontory they beheld her mangled body,
stretched on the blood-stained rocks, whilst the advancing tide was floating her long matted locks and
shattered skull. Her faithful dog was moaning over
her and driving away the screaming sea-birds, that
had already flocked around her to claim their prey.

THE EXILE.

BY W. O. M'NEILSON.

Oh Erin, my home—brightest isle of the ocean!
So calmly reposing upon the dark wave:
So peaceful amid the wild billow's commotion,
Blest home of my childhood! the land of the brave.

Yes—the land of the brave—though a tyrant rules
   o'er thee
Though thy sons, the cold hand of oppression must
   feel:
There is many a heart, that will ever deplore thee;
Wounds, still warmly bleeding, which never will
   heal.

There are bosoms as free, as the air they are breath-
   ing,
And heart's that are panting for liberty's call,
Who would rush like the blue waves, which round
   them are wreathing,
And whelm the oppressors, or gloriously fall.

If the ensign of freedom was over thee waving—
  If some would the long conceal'd banner, unfurl;
There are those who would glory, oppression in
    braving,
  And swift from his station the tyrant would hurl.

And now, undiscover'd, some star may be rising,
From liberty's ocean, to beam on thy shore!
Some firm heart, who Britain's proud tyrant des-
  pising,
Shall speak—and the bondage of Erin, be o'er.

Dear home of my youth, shall I never behold thee?
Nor you, O my loved ones! the joy of my heart;
No more shall these arms to my bosom enfold you!
No more will my light be the smiles you impart!

Oh, never again, mid thy sweet blooming bowers,
At eve, with my heart's dearest joy, will I stray!
Oh! never again, in the morning's first hours,
With her, shall I hail the bright ruler of day!

Now, to my full bosom, eve gathers in sadness
My thoughts all rush back to my dear island home:
And morning flings o'er me, no feeling of gladness,
For far from my country, and lov'd ones, I roam.

STANZAS.

BY MENTOR.

The spot I love is a valley deep,—
Where streams in sparkling cascades leap;
Where echo faintly hears the call,
Giv'n by the tiny waterfall;
Where bowing sweet briars kiss the ground,
And fill the air with fragrance round;
Where sweetest flowers bestrew the dale,
And amorous woodbine wooes the gale.

The hour I love is when evening gray,
Her mantle spreads at close of day,
When the solar ray has ceas'd to beam,
And the western sky has lost its gleam;
When the queen of night has just been crown'd;
And stars resplendent shine around;
And the breeze that through the rosy bower
Had stolen, is hush'd in that still hour.
There is one with whom I 'd love to stray,
In that sweet vale from care away;

When the bee has clos'd his busy wing,
And is heard the streamlet's murmuring,
That in the moon-beam glides along,
Humming its sweetly pensive song.
'Tis thou who in that vale should be
Mary! in that lone hour with me.

FRIENDSHIP.

WHEN the wintry storms of fate,
  Our flowery prospects desolate,
Friendship, like an evergreen,
  Virid 'mid the waste is seen.

When despair with ebon clouds
  In thick gloom our heaven enshrouds;
Friendship's star from the dark sky
  Beams with cheering brilliancy.

TO ELOISE.

BY ALLAN REYNE.

FAREWELL dear girl! for still thy bosom's heaving
   Tells of a something that doth make thee dear;
Farewell dear girl! thy smiles have been deceiving,
   Thy coldness soon will render lone and drear,
The heart, thou oft hast cheer'd as love is wont to
     cheer.

Farewell! the day is gone, alas! forever,
   When it was thine this bosom to have bless'd;
Farewell! the deed is done, that hence must sever
   Me from the maiden on whose snowy breast,
My head has oft reclin'd in more than heavenly
     rest.

Farewell! a last and fond farewell is given—
   Oh! how I've lov'd thee, I may love thee still—
Oft when the sun is sunken low at even
   I'll think of hours, when roving by the rill,
Our mutual hearts have felt affection's genial thrill.

TAHLOOSIN.

Lith. of Endicott & Swett.

THE CURSE OF TAHLOOSIN.

BY J. H. HEWITT.

"Look, Azula, bright-eyed daughter of Tahloosin, the mighty waters are heaving with the canoes
of the proud chief of the Oneidas—he is coming
with his bow unstrung and the pipe of peace in his
right hand. Can Ontwa behold this and his heart
be glad? Can he forsake the lamb while the wings
of the vulture are spreading over it? Go, Azula,
thy father tarries for thee at the door of his wigwam—thou art for Yacochin, the mighty of the
Oneidas."

Thus spake Ontwa to the maid who hung upon
his neck, as if in parting with him she lost her only
stay to existence. "Can the young vine leave the
strong trunk around which it has clung alike
through storms and sunshine?" asked she, fixing her
dark eyes upon his clouded features, "bid the fish
forsake the sparkling sea—the birds the air—the

R

timid deer the deep and silent woods she loves to
hide herself in; but tell not Azula to go from
Ontwa. The winds blow here and there, and shake
at the same time the pine and the maple, and all
the trees of the forest—the bright moon looks
smilingly upon many a brook; but Azula has but
one love—can Ontwa say it is not him? Yacochin,
the chief of the Oneidas has seen many summers,
he has many wives—Azula cannot love him."

"Maiden of the lynx-eye—the word is spoken,"
replied the young warrior, half smiling as he gazed
upon the fond one who clung nearer to him,
"Ontwa is the foe of Yacochin; my bow-string shall
be drawn tight—I will put on my war-belt, and my
foot shall never tire, nor my arm rest until I meet
the chief of Oneida in the strength of battle.—
Azula! thy father is feeble and old, his gray hairs
hang like the bleached moss upon the mournful
cypress, his footsteps falter and his eye is dim.—
Yacochin has rich hunting grounds, food grows in
his fields, his warriors are renowned, and his arm
mighty in strife. Will not Tahloosin give away his
child to the Oneida chief, that his old days may be
the days of peace, and the song of sorrow be sung
over his grave?"

"Ontwa!—the great spirit will be with us— Tahloosin is old but he loves his child for the sake of her mother, whose skin was as fair as the blossom of the dog-wood. He has often told me that the smile of the fair-skinned maiden hung upon my lips, and that my hair was as soft as the silk that shoots from the green maize. Tahloosin will not give his daughter to the man she cannot love."

Ontwa again looked upon the waters of the lake; the fleet of canoes had arrived within a short distance of the shore, and the valley beneath echoed with the wild notes of the conch-shell. A dark and foreboding cloud spread over his brow—his chest heaved like the surface of a troubled sea, and his hand fell involuntarily upon the bright knife that glistened in his leathern belt. Azula watched the various changes of his countenance, and throwing herself again upon his neck, exclaimed. "Does Ontwa doubt Azula?"

"Thou art the offspring of a treacherous and fickle race—the blood of the white man runs in thy veins—Swear, Azula, by the great spirit who now beholds us—whose eye is seen amid the bright lightning, and whose voice is heard in the bursting of the storm-cloud, swear never to be Yacochin's."

The offended girl strove in vain to smother her feelings; tearing herself from the embrace of the young warrior, and standing erect in all the majesty of her nature, she stretched her arm over toward the village at the foot of the mountain.

"Azula needs no oath to bind her faith," said she; "there's her sire's wigwam; will Ontwa go with her to the chief bent down by the weight of many winters?"

"It is enough," returned Ontwa, "take this shell, three long blasts will summon me. Go meet the proud chief, the knife and the hatchet shall be red, for Azula shall never be the wife of Yacochin."

The maid leapt from rock to rock, and tarried not until she reached the village. The council-fires were blazing, and the chiefs and veteran warriors had met—among them sat the aged Tahloosin, the revered and venerated of the tribe; he arose and addressed the assembly:—

"Brothers and chiefs, it has pleased the great spirit to heap upon my head the white snow of sixty winters; I was born among you and have always lived with you—may it also please him who rules the land and the sea, and who guides the winds and the mighty storm, to permit me to die among you. I have fought the battles of my tribe —sixty scalps hang in my wigwam, and my knife is red with the blood of the white man. When the fair sky of youth was over me, and my arm was strong in the midst of the battle, I took the young daughter of a pale-face from the flames of her father's hut; she was fair, as the morning-star, and I brought her to our village. The seasons passed over, the green grass came and went, and the young tree shot up toward the clouds—the fair-skinned maiden grew in years, and I took her for my wife. But she passed away like a tender flower before the cold winds of the north, and left me Azula.— I have watched the bud—I have seen it blossom and ripen, and I have trembled lest *it too* should be taken from me. Chiefs and brethren! the mighty Yacochin comes to claim her hand; I have ruled over you in war and peace, and my weary limbs now long to be resting beneath the sod where sleep the bones of my fathers. Shall Azula be the wife of Oneida's chief?"

R*

Each member of the council gave his assent by a
sedate nod of the head, and the body arose to greet
the Oneidas, whose canoes had just stranded upon
the yellow shore.

Yacochin was received with pomp: He cast a
careless glance upon the beautiful Azula as she
tremblingly handed him a pipe by her father's
commands. There was a coldness in his looks,
which only tended to strengthen her dislike; he had
passed the meridian of life, the frost of age already
began to show itself upon his brow; and, but for
his strong and muscular frame, which is always
fascinating to an Indian's eye, he might have been
called an ugly man. The poor girl's heart was
ready to burst; she dared not encounter the frown
of her father, and yet she knew she must reject the
suit of the Oneida. There was but one course to
pursue, brave the worst and fly with Ontwa.

The next day preparations were made for the
marriage ceremony; the women and the warriors
were gathered around the wigwam of the aged
chief, and Azula tremblingly sought her father's
resence. "Tahloosin!—Brave in war and wise in
peace," said she throwing her arms tenderly around

the neck of the old man, "Azula is come to take a heavy load from her heart. Thou art my sire— and hast said that thou lovest me. Would Tahloosin throw a tender fawn to the hungry wolf?— Would he give the dove to the talons of the hawk?"

The old chief only knit his brow in reply to his weeping daughter—the truth flashed upon his mind, she was determined to thwart his intentions, and bring sorrow upon his declining years. "Azula," said he glancing fiercely upon the downcast maiden —"thou wert the prop of my old age. Shall the sun set amidst the storm clouds—shall thy father tear his grey hairs and scatter them on the four winds of the heavens? Look up—the nuptial fire is kindled before our wigwam, and the chief of the Oneidas awaits thy coming."

"Father!—as the hoar rock is dear to the young vine, so thou art to me—but, by the great spirit who can hear the whisperings of the summer winds upon the bosom of the waters, I cannot give my heart to Yacochin."

The eyes of the hoary chief flashed fire; he cast his daughter from him, and, stretching his arms wide, exclaimed;—"The curse of Tahloosin be upon thee—the clinging curse of a father upon his offspring, if thou art opposed to his dearest hopes! May the wrathful fires of heaven fall upon thy head, and consume thee, if thou lovest another than Yacochin; may the cavern of damned spirits be too narrow and its flames too shallow for thine accursed soul to revel in.   Azula!—come to the nuptial feast—or be this thy doom!"

Saying this he left the trembling girl, and joined those who were awaiting the appearance of the bride in front of the wigwam.   Azula, scarcely knowing what she did, sped to the rock on which she had the day before parted with Ontwa.   Thrice she blew the shell, and the echo rolled along the valley —In a moment the young warrior was by her side.

"Ontwa!"—said she, "I will bear the curse of Tahloosin for thee.   Let us fly, there are lands beyond the waters where we can live—love like that I bear for thee can bring happiness to the wilderness."

"Dear Azula,—my arm is strong and my canoe is swift.   Follow my footsteps, I will lead thee to the waters."

They had scarcely commenced descending the rocky slope, when the wild notes of the conch-shell echoed through the valley, and the yells of pursuers were heard louder and louder. Ontwa hurried Azula along from rock to rock, and through brake and fen until they reached the shore.

The frowning aspect of the heavens was painted with still blacker hues upon the awfully still bosom of the stream; the rocks hung darkly over its high banks, and the low muttering of the gathering clouds, caused the lovers to hesitate a moment ere they entered their frail bark.

"The wrath of the great spirit is upon us," said Azula, looking fearfully toward the vapours as they slowly and heavily gathered over their heads.— "The curse of Tahloosin is upon me—Ontwa! let us return."

"Faint-hearted Azula!—the waters and the winds and the storm-clouds are nothing to the rage of an offended father. Wouldst thou return *now*? Be it so—go and forget Ontwa, if thou canst, he alone will brave the tempest."

The young girl threw herself upon his bosom, and then seizing his hand, exclaimed—"Ontwa shall not go alone—death with him were better than life with Yacochin!"

They leapt into the canoe and pushed it from the land just as a body of their pursuers reached the rocks above them. The aged Tahloosin who stood upon an advanced rock breasting the wind which now began to blow furiously—saw his only child borne away by the man whom he hated, and stretching his boney arms over the deep; he again called the vengeance of the great spirit down upon them. Azula waved a farewell to her angry sire, while Ontwa with a desperate hope paddled the light canoe over the heavy waves that endeavored in vain to bar their way. They were just clearing the point which obstructed their view of the village, when they observed for the first time that they were pursued by a fleet of canoes. Azula shrieked when she saw that Yacochin and two other indians occupied the foremost—seizing a paddle she encouraged her lover in his exertions, and for a long time they confronted the raging elements.

The Oneidas gained upon them, in spite of their efforts—the storm raged high, and both boats were making fast toward the rapids. Ontwa still labored with all his remaining strength, but his paddle fell from his hand, and he uttered a wild shriek of despair, when he saw poor Azula fall to the bottom of the canoe with the arrow of Yacochin rankling in her heart! She turned her full dark eyes upon him with an expression which he could not but understand, and sighed out her spirit. "Daughter of the fair-skinned—Azula!" exclaimed the lover bitterly —"we will not be long apart; there are happy places in the land of departed spirits, for those who have loved." Suddenly his features became clouded, he seized his bow, and tearing the shaft from the breast of the dead maiden, winged it back to the heart of the infernal chief!

The two remaining Oneidas when they saw their chief fall like a mass of lead into the turbulent deep, uttered a loud yell, and pushed their canoe, by several quick strokes of the paddle, directly by the side of that of Ontwa, who, with one blow of his tommahawk severed the skull of the nearest.— The other immediately grappled with him, and the struggle was long and fearful, each endeavoring to throw the other from his foot-hold. The storm continued to rage—the roar of the mighty cataract now began to add to the horror of the scene—the waves tossed as if battling with the clouds, and the canoes of the struggling warriors rapidly floated toward the yawning gulph. "Azula! Azula!—I am coming!"—shouted Ontwa as the boats plunged over the foaming verge. Down—down the horrid abyss they went, joining their wild yell with the roar of the waters. The storm rolled on, the water spirit shrieked amid the deafening tumult—the canoes floated along through the curling eddies, but the warriors were seen no more.

THE FIRE AT SEA.

The wind is fair, "hoist sails, the anchor weigh!"
Pelion commands, the active tars obey;
O'er the green waves the ship majestic rides,
Like the proud eagle through the azure glides;
With swelling sails she leaves the busy port,
Hope fills each breast, elate each sailor's heart.
Aseneth fair, bound for Britania's climes,
With generous Alfred on the stern reclines,
And Gilbert brave, Columbia's worthy son;
Ennobled by deeds for Britain won,
Now parting from his native land once more
To reap fresh laurels on proud Albion's shore.
Bright prospects cheer, fair scenes before them lay,
E'en nature bids them speed upon their way;
No angry clouds along th' horizon scowl,
No tempests nurs'd in ocean's bosom howl,
Through tranquil skies, light's sacred fountain pours
The flood of day, o'er seas and verdant shores.

How mutable earth's scenes! for scarce the sun,
Two daily trips through heaven's bright vault had
     run—
E'er clouds envelope, blustering winds arise;
And tempests murmur in the thick'ning skies:
The madden'd seas, their foaming arms extend
Dripping with spray, and plash the vessel's bend;
Swelling with rage, they break with sullen power
High o'er her sides, and dash the briny shower;
Loud through the rigging howls the rushing wind,
The surging billows, urg'd by those behind,
Now rock the ship upon the mountain wave,
Then deep engulph her where the waters rave.
The fall of night portends th' approaching war
Of marshall'd elements, when from afar
In western skies the storm-cloud rears its head—
Its eyes flash lightning from the ocean's bed,
And weep in torrents, while its troubled breath
Disturbs the deep and sounds the blast of death.
How fearful its approach!   The awful roll
Of coming thunder speaks from pole to pole,
Deep and more dense roll on the gloomy clouds
Egyptian darkness, sea and heaven enshrouds;
Save as the lightning shedding vivid rays,

Darting in forky streams unceasing plays;
Fierce blows the wind, the mingled torrent pours,
Thick fly the shafts, the dreadful thunder roars;
On the mast head, where signals proudly stream,
The angry spirits of the deep are seen;
The trembling mariners foreboding stand,
Pelion compos'd, regards, and gives command—
"Lash to the helm!" when a fierce hissing flash!
Falls on the ship with most tremendous crash
Two are struck low, cold horror seiz'd the crew;
The electric matter through the vessel flew;
All rush on deck in terror and alarm,
Aseneth trembling—eyes the raging storm!
Her gentle bosom heav'd a boding sigh,
At the wild conflict of the sea and sky:
Alfred with all a brother's fondness tries,
To soothe her grief—what means that crackling
      noise?
"The ship's on fire!" th' appalling cry is heard,
With agonizing shock by all on board.
They raise the hatches! cut away the decks—
Stave in the casks! but nought its fury checks—
"Out with the boats!" then Pelion loud exclaims—
"All! all is lost! no other hope remains!"

The redd'ning flames burst frightful from the hold!
Volumes of smoke and fire terrific roll'd—
Crack up the masts, on sails and rigging seize,
And wrap the ship in one heart-rending blaze.
Th' expansive lightning mingles with the glow
Of burning timbers—sparks fly thick below
And meet the sparks above—the lurid glare
Gilds the dark clouds, and lights the smoky air.
In two frail boats, without provision cast,
Scorch'd by the sun—expos'd to every blast:
Lost and undone, their wretched, suffering state,
Soon seal'd the delicate Aseneth's fate!
Wrapp'd in a cloak, her head reclining lay,
On the hard boards, life sinking fast away,
A heavenly smile calm resignation shed,
For virtue rallied all her cheering-aid:
Amid the trying scene, yet e'er the stroke
Of death had pierc'd, she thus to Alfred spoke:—
"Oh! cease thy weeping brother! dry thy tears—
My dying heart will soon forget its fears;
No more shall sorrow wring this aching breast,
Borne to the mansions of eternal rest,
Nothing on earth deserves my longer stay—
Why keep my spirit from its God away?"

"Aseneth dear! and must I from thee part?
Must the wide ocean tear thee from my heart?
How can my soul support the loss of thee?
Thus doubly press'd by grief and misery."
Not the stern Gilbert, (whose courageous heart,
In midst of battle bore the hero's part,
When ship by ship in fierce encounter hung,
And ocean's caves from murderous cannon rung)
E'er felt such sorrow touch his feeling breast,
As when the dying girl's cold hand he press'd.
Soft melting tears stole down each sailor's cheek,
As her warm thanks she faintly sought to speak:
And e'er night's dusky curtains spread the deep,
In Alfred's arms she sweetly sank to sleep.

Thus heedless strays from Yemen's happy vales,
Some cherish'd bird, borne on the spicy gales;
Caught by the samiel o'er the desert lands
'Tis lost and buried in the burning sands.

What though no sable trapping grace thy bier?
No pompous hearse doth dark with plumes appear,
No friends assembled for a funeral ride,
While slow-drawn coaches form the train of pride.

s*

Yet heart-felt tears from lorn companions fell
As the wild sea-bird shriek'd thy mournful knell;
With fervent prayer, and sacred rites they gave,
Thy decent body to its liquid grave.
There rest in peace the billow is thy shroud,
Thy dirge, the awful accents of the cloud,
When tempests rush above thy holy bed,
And there shall sea-nymphs coral branches spread,
Upon thy tomb, and strew with beauteous shells,
And pearly garlands brought from chrystal wells;
Till future times and ages pass away,
And God's dread voice calls forth thy sleeping clay.

J. O.

RUINS.

I've stood amid the mouldering piles
Of Grecian fanes in ruins laid;
I've wept among the desert aisles
Where blooming Art and Science stray'd.

I've seen the twining ivy wind
'Mid Balbec and Palmyra's halls;
And weeping strode among the wastes
Of Babylon's infested walls.

I've pour'd a tide of sorrow where
The fierce volcano roll'd along
Its fiery waves and cities whelm'd
Beneath its inundation strong.

But ne'er did fane or cities waste
Such sick'ning sorrow o'er impart
As when I've seen the ruins dire
Of trusting woman's broken heart.

N. C.

THE HERMIT.

BY P. C. DORAN.

Bless'd memory, guide, with finger nicely true
Back to my youth my retrospective view.

KIRK WHITE.

It was a cold night in December, when Merlin sitting in his neat cottage parlor, watching the dying embers of the fire, was summoned to the door by a knock. A visit at this time of night was unusual, thought Merlin, yet it might be some of the neighbors, who were in need of assistance, and the door of the "Green Cottage" was never closed against the necessitous. With the timidity of advanced age, but with the fearlessness of honesty, he approached the door, and demanded who was there?

"One," replied a faltering voice, "who has need of your assistance—the Hermit."

"What! the recluse of Trevin hill."

"The same," replied he.

Merlin, who had never seen the Hermit, as he was called, and had long wished for an opportunity to converse with him, on the impulse of the moment opened the door, the moon shone bright, and fell full upon the features of the Hermit, betraying a man far advanced in years, with a countenance pale, almost ghastly, large dark eyes, and hair white as the fleecy clouds, falling over his neck in luxuriance. Merlin stepped back with surprise, and raising his eyes to the face of the stranger met the look of the Hermit—it was enough, the majestic brow, the aqueline nose and the black expressive eye, told him it was the friend of his youth, Carlin S———.

"Do I find a welcome?" asked the intruder, as Merlin stood gazing with astonishment.

"A welcome!" exclaimed he, roused from his trance. "Can Carlin think for an instant my door would be closed when he demanded entrance.— Come in, and share with me my all!"

"Then I have one friend, and I may die content. Let me embrace thee; it is long, since these arms have twined round a human being, and now my almost frozen heart beats again with the throb of joy."

"Merlin" said the Hermit, "this is the first time for years that I have stood beneath a roof made by mortal hands; my bed has been the earth, my covering the sky, and in yonder cave, I sought seclusion from the world. Perhaps I should not so soon have sought society, and held communion with my kind, had not each succeeding day told me, I was fast leaving behind me all my sorrows, and that I should prepare to die. Those who have always lived among the friends of their infancy, and never been tossed on the troubled ocean of life, cannot even fancy that when in the solitude of the forest, man endeavors to shun man, how 'heart speaks to heart' —how his soul yearns to find one, with whom he may converse; but the victim of misfortune will shrink from that communion. He has trusted many and found them "wanting," and he hates—he despises *all*.

"It was so with me. I need not tell you how many have benefitted by my bounty, and that I have ever refused favors, whilst I have been an inmate of that cell, you know. But, still, I could not entirely hate mankind though I have long wished to do so. Listen to my story, and then tell me have I not cause?

"Merlin, you were my earliest friend, and it is fit you should hear my history. When we parted at Genoa, you to return to your father and mother, and I to accompany mine to the grave, you held a holy place in my bosom; I loved you with all the ardor of youthful friendship, and knew that you were one in whom I could confide. I believe I can still. But, enough—we parted, and I reached home in time to see the earth close over those who had given me being. I could not live in the place where every thing served to remind me of my loss, and removed to a small farm, situated on the Rhine.— Here I lived three years, when I yielded to the solicitation of an uncle, who resided in Switzerland, in the village of Goldau, where I myself was born, and went to live with him.

"On my journey I was much entertained by the relation of a peasant, who informed me, that on one of the Islands in the Lake of Lowertz, lived a man, who had come there several months before, accompanied by a young girl, said to be his daughter. His simple narrative, and the description he gave of the girl, excited my curiosity, and I determined if possible to visit the place.

"On the evening of the fifth of September, (how fondly memory still clings to that day,) when the sun had left the valley, and was gilding the tops of the mountain with his glory, giving the western sky a grandeur of appearance equalled only by his own —not a leaf was stirred and the waters of the Lowertz reflected the blue vault of heaven, whose clouds wrapped in the purity of the skies, "rested from their labor"—I was startled by a loud shriek that reverberated awfully through the valley and mountain, and on looking up I saw that part of the mountain was falling!

> "Slowly it came in its mountain wrath;
> And the valley vanish'd before its path;
> And the rude cliffs bow'd; and the waters fled;
> And the living were buried; whilst over their head
> They heard the full march of the foe as he sped—
> And the valley of life was the tomb of the dead."

"As I stood gazing on this scene of horror beholding the home of my youth, obliterated from the face of the earth, together with all my kindred; I could

not refrain from tears. I saw men rushing out of
their houses, to meet a more certain destruction,
while the shrieks of women calling for assistance, when none could be given, filled the air.—
The story of the peasant rushed on my mind, and
turning my eyes towards the island, I saw it was
overflown by the earth falling into the lake, and
that the old man was struggling for the shore. I
instantly plunged into the water; a few moments
brought me to him—his head was gray, and the
sinews of his arm were withered—still did he hold
with his hand the body of his daughter. On my
approach his powers relaxed—he uttered a prayer
—and exclaimed, "Save my daughter, save my
Beatrice!" and sank to rise no more. I caught the
fragile form of the fair girl, as she sank—"with
one hand I dashed the saucy waves, that pressed
and thronged to rob me of my prize, and with the
other bore her safely to the shore!"

"What was my surprise, when I discovered it
was Beatrice L———, whom I had seen only once
before, but whom from that hour I had loved. She
recognized me, and never shall I forget the thrill
of joy, with which my bosom swelled, when she
T

thanked me, and observed:—"I have seen those eyes
before,"—the sentence was left unfinished, but the
tear of joy was in her eye, and I read what language failed to express—she loved me.   Merlin,
never did I see one so beautiful—long—long could
I dwell on the theme, but it calls up too many tender recollections, and even now, when my feelings
are frozen and chill, the thought of that moment
brings tears to my eyes, and I am a *man* again.

"We were married, and happiness smiled on our
union, when I found in the person of R———, a
bane to my future joy.   He had been a suitor for
the hand of Beatrice, but she in accordance with
her own sentiments, and the advice of her father,
had rejected him.   His pride was stung, and having
great influence with the government, in which he
was a high officer, he manufactured charges against
old L———, who fled to Switzerland, seeing nought
awaited him, but dishonor, in his native land.   On
the island he remained in security till the mountain
fell, and you know the rest.

"When the monster R———, found Beatrice
was married, and had returned home, he directed
his malice against me.   In vain did I urge my in-

nocence, in vain did I appeal to the justice of my country—I was condemned to banishment, but Beatrice was not to be permitted to accompany me. At this time I was deserted by all mankind; save her, who hung around me like a vine that has wound itself about a feeble oak, that is not able to support it. The thought of leaving her in the power of the monster, almost deprived me of my reason. Those who had heretofore been my friends were now my enemies. Men who before had smiled upon me, now knew me not. I was an outcast among mankind and the finger of scorn was pointed at me. Should I not have hated the world?

"The day soon arrived when I was to leave the land of my fathers, and though during my confinement I had been denied every comfort, I was permitted to see Beatrice once more. How vivid is the scene of our meeting even now! I had not seen her for several days, and oh! how altered—the once bright and glowing girl, presented the pale emaciated form of a being on the verge of existence. I did not weep, for I felt an inward joy that she was passing to heaven, leaving the world which was so unworthy of her. I held her to my bosom, and kissed her fair forehead." Here the Hermit burst into tears, and Merlin was too much affected to interrupt his sorrow. In a short time he recovered himself, and continued his story!

"Excuse this weakness, my friend. These are the first tears I have shed for many a long year, and Beatrice is worthy of them all. As I held her to my bosom, I would not have exchanged her for the wealth of all the world, and yet I was so soon to leave her. The officer reminded me, that the time had come for embarkation. I unloosed my arms, and she gave one wild, long, loud cry—even now it rings in my ears—and fell into my arms—a corpse! Oh! in one short moment, how had my heart become cold! I looked on her, I saw death was on her cheek, and that her spirit had fled, yet I shed no tear—I felt no regret. I looked around, and the eyes of many were on me—joy—heart-felt, thrilling joy burst from my lips—I laughed in ecstacy, for the monster was disappointed!

"From that time, I have shunned all communication with the world, for I had no one to love me, and I thought I hated all men.

"Yesternight, I stood on the bank of the river, looking on the surrounding scene—the chill air swept along the trees of the forest, which were stripped of their foliage, but the waters were not frozen, and lay calmly beneath my feet—the moon at this moment issued from behind a cloud, and I saw reflected in the transparent stream my own figure. My hair was white and my face pale, my eye had lost its fire—death was pictured in every feature. The moon again sunk behind a cloud and left one solitary star shining in the heavens— like me, it had no companion, and it appeared fast waning; as I stood gazing the morning came, and that star was the last to leave the sky.

The wishes which had been intruding on me, now came to my mind. I longed for one on whom I might lay my bosom—I wished for a friend, some one to close my eyes, and to weep over me when dead. You passed from your house just then, and though I had seen you before I did not recognize you till that moment. Merlin, thought I, will perhaps know me, and may still be a friend."

The Hermit again paused, evidently much agitat-

T*

ed, when suddenly starting up, he exclaimed in a tremulous voice:—

"Merlin, look there! Methought Beatrice passed the casement even now, and smiling pointed to that star. It is the one I saw last night. Look at it!—See how fast it wanes. Merlin, my hour is come,—I feel the hand of death is on me. Stop! take this minature, it is Beatrice's; she gave it to me on the day she became mine:—Keep it for my sake, and when I am dead lay me beside the river, let no stone mark the spot where I lie, and ———— but the star is gone!"

Merlin waited for him to proceed but his noble spirit had fled.

VIRTUE.

BY COVINGTON.

When grief her sable pall hath thrown,
O'er all that once in beauty shone;
And cares with gloomy fears combin'd,
Cloud the horizon of the mind,
Oh! I have seen fair Virtue pour
Her rays, and life and light restore.

When vice with pestilential breath
Has breath'd the fumes of moral death,
And sick'ning souls, weak—faint—unsound
Inhale the dire contagion round;
Then have I seen fair Virtue glow
Fresh as the rose—pure as the snow.

When fortunes winds have howl'd aloud,
And storms of fate the heavens enshroud;
And sinking souls with clouds o'ercast
Bend like the ozier 'neath the blast,
I've Virtue seen with aspect bland
Firm as the "rock of ages" stand.

When worldly power has fail'd to bless,
When wealth has lost its usefulness,
When rich and glittering gems, to him
Lorn and distress'd, are poor and dim;
Then, have I seen fair Virtue shine
Resplendent as Golconda's mine.

Oh! Virtue! how serenely sweet,
The graces which in thee do meet.
Thy presence bids all sorrow cease,
Thy look is love, thy smile is peace:
Thou lead'st where endless fountains roll
Their streams of bliss upon the soul.

HOPES.

I'VE seen the waves toss high their foaming crests
In fleecy beauty to the solar gleam,
Then burst and mingle with the ocean's surf;
While others forming from their broken base
Succeed in swelling grandeur to the eye,
And I have said 'tis thus with human hopes,
They rise in beauty on our raptur'd sight,
Then fall, and on their ruins others rise,
Infinite, in successive mockery.

THE SWISS EMIGRANTS.

BY J. C. MONTSERRAT.

HEAR my son, the plashing oar!
Look! the boats forsake the shore;
Weeping mourners crowd the strand,
Soon to quit their fatherland.
Leave the realm of Tyranny!
Seek a home amid the free!
Switzerland is fair to view,
Fair her streams and mountains blue,
Sweet her bright and sunny plains,
Where transporting beauty reigns,
Rich the produce of her soil,
Plenteous flow her wine and oil,
Beauteous are her starry skies,
Brilliant are her maidens' eyes;
But to souls untam'd and free
What are these to Liberty?
Leave thy home, thy purple vines
For the alien canes and pines.

Soon thy sire his race shall run,
Soon thy mother's course be done;
And beside the foaming Rhine,
Will *our* hoary heads recline.
We'd not have *our children's* graves
In a land of crouching slaves.
Leave the realm of Tyranny!
Seek a home amid the free!
To thy fond, fraternal care,
I confide thy sister dear.
Should the thought her bosom swell
Of the home she lov'd so well;
And the gathering tear confess
The weary exile's loneliness,
Cheer her gloom; in sympathy
A father—mother—brother be.
Hear oh Heaven! a father's prayer,
See a yearning mother's tear,
Shield our offspring guard and guide
O'er the broad Atlantic tide.

LOVE BETRAYED.

BY CONSTANTINE.

Soft vernal showers may, to the faded fields,
Restore their verdant robes of pristine beauty;
Southern winds may breathe upon the rose-tree,
And diffuse the blushing buds o'er its dead boughs;
The naked groves assume their leaves, and streams
Of melody from sylvan songsters roll,
In tides of rapture o'er the verdant plains;
Where wintery desolation mute did reign.
The waning moon that sheds her obtuse rays
Glimm'ring through Heaven, may again repair
Her fading light, and the great orb of day,
That sinking gleams upon the western verge,
Shine with augmented brightness on the morrow.
        But alas!
There is no power can bid the faded soul
Of love betray'd, bloom with its former grace,
Or wake one joyful strain where damp despair
Has rusted every fibre of the soul,
Or wake one smile, where desolation dark
Enwraps the spirit in Cimmerian gloom.

CHARLES MORAY.

BY ROBERT CAREY.

CHARLES MORAY was descended from an ancient
family in England, which from the earliest days of
that nation had been celebrated for its loyalty.——
His father, a man of an ambitious and active temper, had unfortunately engaged in an unsuccessful
attempt against the power of the reigning monarch,
for which offence his estates were taken away
from his family and he himself sent into exile,
where, after some years of wandering and wretchedness, he died in an obscure place, the victim of
want and disease. Charles Moray in consequence
of the misdeeds of his father, found himself, at
the age of twenty, without any hopes of prefer-
ment in his own country, shunned by those
whom he had once known, and neglected by all.——
Inheriting the bold and ambitious spirit of his father, with a great degree of that pride which be-
longs to those of an aspiring and lofty character,

and seeing that on account of the disadvantage under which he labored, so long as he remained in his own country, there were no hopes of his ever rising to eminence, he collected whatever articles of value he had, with the determination of leaving forever the land that had given him birth. Accordingly, as soon as his arrangements were effected, he embarked for the continent of Europe, with the intention of wandering over it, until he should fall in with some warlike noble, in whose ranks he might find promotion. He hoped by this means, to be able speedily to rise into distinction, for he rightly judged, that in those days, when wars constituted almost the constant occupation of life, the camp afforded a great field for one of a bold and determined character to rise into power and importance. With this design, after having landed upon the coast of France, he set forward with nothing but a robust constitution, and a bold heart, to aid him in the toils and difficulties he was about to encounter. His feelings were for a long time not of the most enviable kind. Of a warm and enthusiastic temperament, he felt a strong attachment to his native land; and now that he was

V

leaving that land forever, the bitterness of his thoughts became almost insupportable to him.—— Several times he was on the point of retracing his steps, but the reflection of the disadvantage he laboured under at home always urged him to continue onward. He reflected that his own country had no longer any allurements for him, and that as long as he remained in it, he would be noticed only as the son of one who had violated that great obligation, which every man is under, to support the government under which he lives. To be known merely as an object of curiosity, to be pointed out as one upon whose name disgrace had been stamped, was so galling a thought to him, that in the contemplation of it, the bitterness of his feelings, which grew out of his attachment to his country, soon began to wear off. By degrees he came to look with more of composure upon his fortune, until at last he entirely forgot its hardships; and set vigorously to work in the accomplishment of his design of raising the fallen name he inherited.

To one of this bold, enterprising, and determined character, there was in those days every chance of success in life. The camp itself, as we have already said, opened a great field for one of such a character. But this was not the only path in which our young adventurer determined to follow. In his own country he had devoted much of his attention to the political affairs of the times; he had watched the course of events, narrowly, and had in fact, laid a foundation for that fame, which, in after years, he acquired, as a great statesman.

    *   *   *   *   *

It was now about two years after Charles Moray had landed upon the shores of France, on a beautiful summer's day, that a number of persons were seen travelling along the banks of a river in the valley of Lorraine, which was one of the most beautiful regions in all the south of France.— Among these travellers there was a lady of extreme youth and beauty, who rode gracefully upon a gay and shewy steed; and by her side a young cavalier of rather a tall and slight, though muscular figure, who seemed disposed to shew the lady all the attention that a gallant could shew a maiden. The young man's appearance was uncommonly fine and striking. The flush of health was upon his cheek, and his long black hair hung down gracefully from underneath his cap, which was so placed upon his head as to display a beautiful and strongly marked forehead. His eyes were dark and sparkling, and betokened fire of soul, and energy of character, with a spirit that would be indomitable in fight. These two personages were the lady Ellen of Lorraine, the daughter of the Duke of that name, and our adventurer Charles Moray, who some eighteen or twenty months before had found his way into the ranks of the Duke. The rest of the party consisted of the Duke himself with several knights, and a number of retainers, who were returning home from a visit to the court of their monarch, where for some time past there had been held a grand festival at which all the nobles and distinguished of the nation were present. Charles, who had been at this festival among the rest, had received from the monarch of France, whilst at the court, the honours of knighthood—these were bestowed upon him for his prowess and skilful conduct in a late war, in which he had engaged as a follower of the Duke of Lorraine. The Duke was now only a short distance from his castle, and had been travelling for some weeks, during which time he had encountered several dangers. Once in travelling through a wild and mountainous country, his party had been attacked by robbers, bands of whom at that time infested all the forests of France, Italy, Spain and Germany. During this attack Charles Moray had freed the lady Ellen from the hands of two of the ruffians, just as they were about to bear her away to some of their lurking places; and had assisted greatly in otherwise resisting and dispersing them. On other occasions too, of danger, he had evinced great courage, and disregard of danger, for which he had gained great favor, not only with the Duke himself, but also with the lady Ellen.

The party now arrived at the castle, where the time passed by in a continual round of pleasure and amusement for some months. During this time Ellen's feelings towards Charles Moray, which at first had been but those of esteem and admiration, began to partake somewhat of a warmer character. They were now often together. Indeed our hero seemed to find no pleasure any where else than in her company; for the pleasures
v*

of the chase and the other active amusements of those times, he had deserted entirely, and was only to be seen, either rambling with the fair object of his love, or wandering by himself in those solitary, secluded places, where he supposed no one would observe him.

These circumstances however, did not seem to excite any great attention on the part of the inmates of the castle, for they never dreamed even for a moment, that there was any thing like a feeling of love, entertained by either Moray or Ellen. It was true, they saw them much together, yet they supposed his accompanying Ellen in her walks nothing more than an act of mere courtesy: besides, too, the difference of situation precluded all ideas of this sort from their minds. The one, the daughter of one of the most powerful nobles of the age, to whose hand even the highest of the land might be suitors; and the other a stranger, whose origin was unknown, except as it was revealed by himself, and one who at all events appeared in the light of an adventurer, whom chance had thrown into his present situation. But though Ellen saw in Charles Moray, a stranger, an adven-

turer, whom chance had thrown in her way, yet
still she regarded him in another light than this.
She looked upon him as one who had in all proba-
bility saved her life, and for this she felt grateful;
she admired the bold determined spirit, the fearlessness of danger, which he had several times dis-
played-in giving assistance to those who were in
peril. Besides she saw in him an accomplished
gentleman, of a beautiful and manly figure, rich in
all the graces of person, which things are never
without their weight in a maiden's estimation of
character; and which are always sure to raise, at
least, admiration, in a woman's breast. The tran-
sition then from admiration is easy and quick: after it comes liking, then approving, and finally that
all-absorbing feeling of love, which when once felt
shuts out all considerations of prudence as to the
origin, character or situation of those for whom
it is felt. It is the great master passion of a
young woman's heart, and exercises uncontrolled
power over all her actions.

The feeling entertained at this time, by the lady
Ellen for Charles Moray, was not yet that of love,
but it soon became so. They were sitting one even-

ing upon the banks of the river that made its way around the castle, when a conversation ensued between them, in which our hero related to Ellen his whole history, the family from which he was descended, the death of his 'father, the evils he endured in his own country, the determination he made to leave it, and in fact all the particulars of his life up to the present time. During this conversation it was that Ellen's feelings towards our hero were ripened into those of love. The generous bearing and high courage he had already displayed, had created in her breast admiration and regard; and now that she had heard the story of his sufferings, like Desdamona, she loved him for the dangers he had braved.

＊　　　＊　　　＊　　　＊　　　＊

The castle of Lord Henry of Lorraine, was situated in the midst of a broad and beautiful plain, surrounded on two sides by high mountains, with a view of the sea which at some distance off spread its broad expanse of waters far as the eye could reach. It was a building of the gothic order, somewhat flat in the middle, with tall spiral towers at each side. The windows were painted as was the fashion of those times, with various colours, resembling the many tints of the forest in autumn; and the whole structure presented one of the most beautiful sights of the sort that those times afforded.

It was now about the commencement of the autumn of the year, two years; after the events described in the preceding part of this narrative had taken place, that the inmates of this castle were seen upon its turrets, looking anxiously along the plain that spread itself broad and far before them. The most conspicuous among these was a female, whose beauty was perfect as that of a full blossomed rose:—she was rich and voluptuous in appearance as is the grape that hangs upon the vine, ready to be plucked. Expectation was strongly marked upon her face, mingled with hope and traces of anxiety. She had a calm, light blue eye—the eye of softness and of love; and her cheek was tinged with the flush of health. This was the lady Ellen of Lorraine, the same whom two years before we have described as very young travelling through a wild country, with a certain Charles Moray, who had afterwards been blessed with her love. She was then but a girl, a warm, generous, unskilled girl, just ripening into womanhood. Now she was a full grown woman, with all the charms and imposing beauties of maturer years.

The Duke of Lorraine, her father, was one of those nobles who delighted in the wars, that were carried on by his monarch, and was consequently always eager to lend his presence and his power, whenever there was the least occasion or demand for either. He had been for some time absent on an expedition of a warlike nature, and was now returning to his castle, after having assisted in achieving a great victory over the enemies of his monarch. A messenger had been sent before to inform his household of his approach, and also with directions that the castle should be put in readiness for the reception of a large number of guests, as he had with him besides his own followers a number of knights, who in returning from battle had taken advantage of the escort afforded them by his train. Besides, too, it was the fashion of those days that after a battle there should always be a feast. A soldier is ever the fondest of the pleasures of conviviality. His life being one of danger, toil, hardships and privations, whilst in the camp, it is but natural to suppose that he would eagerly seize upon the pleasures of the court, whenever he found a respite from the field.

It was now the time that the Duke and his band were expected, and the lady Ellen and others of the castle and its dependencies, were watching eagerly as we have described, from the turrets of the castle to get the first glimpse of the approaching warriors. They had now been gazing for some time along the plain, and were about to descend, supposing that some accident had happened to delay their return, when the distant sounds of martial music broke softly and faintly on the ear, and tall plumes and banners were soon seen waving in the air, and the sounds of the music grew louder and louder until Ellen could distinctly hear the song, that the warriors of her country always sung, when returning home from the field of battle. It was the song of her nation, and like the national airs of the present day, was never heard without awakening those patriotic feelings, which have their existence in every one's heart. The band was now so near that Ellen could plainly distin-

guish the tall person of her father as he rode ma-
jestically at the head of his followers. Her quick
glance too soon discovered the badge and bearing
of one, whose return was a subject of no less joy
to her than that of her father. This was a knight
of handsome appearance, who rode on the right
hand of the Duke, a circumstance indicating him to
be one of the most distinguished of the train.—
Ellen soon fixed her glance upon this person, and
as she did so joy might be seen to sparkle in her
eye, and gladness to manifest itself in all her actions.

The setting sun had tinged the clouds that were
scattered about the west with crimson and gold.—
The long shadows of the evening gave additional
beauty to the scenery of the plain, while to render
the prospect still more imposing, rode this magnificent band of armed warriors, whose brazen helmets,
steel bucklers and cuirasses, glittered in the sunbeams as they moved along. The warriors came
slowly on, keeping time to the notes of the music
as they marched; suddenly they turned around a
point in the road, and as they did so the sounds of
the clarion, the horn, and the many other instru-

ments of those days, burst upon the ears of those
within the castle in one loud swell, which reverberated throughout its multitudinous apartments.—
At this moment the drawbridge was let down, and
the portcullis raised, when the whole band, horsemen and foot, marched over into the court yard.—
And now was presented a scene of some confusion.
The horsemen had dismounted, and the whole party were scattered about, horses and men, knights
and vassals, indiscriminately. They were dispersed in groups, some talking together earnestly,
others grasping each other's hands; menials were
hastening here and there; some ushering the nobles
of the party into the hall, and others eagerly inquiring after their fellows who had gone in the
ranks to battle. Such was the scene of bustle and
commotion in the court-yard. But whilst all this
was enacting there, a scene of quite a different
character, was passing within the castle. Before
scarcely any of the party had dismounted, Charles
Moray (whom we have alluded to, as the person
who rode at the right hand of the Duke, and upon
whom the lady Ellen had fixed her gaze from the
tops of the castle) had found his way into the hall,

W

where meeting Ellen alone, they were wrapped in each other's embrace, for the first time, after a separation of years. This was the sweetest, happiest hour of their existence,—all the anxieties, the doubts, the fears of danger, that once harrowed up their souls, were forgotten in that moment of voiceless rapture. Life even in its brightest moments has no joy like this. The patriot in the hour of his triumph, surrounded by his grateful and applauding countrymen, the warrior in the heat and excitement of the battle, the prisoner released from his long-borne chains,—none of these feel a joy like that of lovers, who, young and ardent, meet after a separation of years of uncertainty and danger.

Some two or three hours had now elapsed since the arrival of the Duke and his followers, when all, both lords and ladies, were assembled in the banquet hall. The knights had laid aside their rough and ponderous armor, and had substituted in its place the rich and shewy court dress; and the ladies had arrayed themselves for the occasion in the rich silks of their country, the manufacture of which had commenced a short time previous.—

The Duke sat at the head of the board; the nobles of the company being seated near him on each side, whilst those who were inferiors in rank, such as gentlemen retainers and strangers of like degree, were seated "below the salts." This part of the table "below the salts," (as it has been jestingly distinguished) was generally the merriest end of the board, at all feasts in those days, for the humorous, the gay, the careless half-dissipated, poor gentlemen of the times, always sat at this end, which was generally kept in continual merriment by the bright sallies and happy retorts of these merry, though rather badly used sons of poverty. Among those *below the salts* on this occasion, was a little man, of whom we will have to take some more particular notice, than of the rest of those around him. He was a thin, care-worn looking personage, of short statue, and exceeding delicate frame. He had light hair, which hung down in long locks about his head, and half concealed, half disclosed to view, a high and impending forehead. His eyes, which he moved quickly from side to side, as if watching every movement of those around him, were sunk deep in his head, and were unusually small in size, and uncommonly dark in color. He was one whom from his entire appearance, at first glance, you would pronounce a deep, treacherous, artful, wily villian. The sinister expression of his eye, its quick, hawk-like glances, the scowl that was ever upon his brow, the care-worn face and attenuated figure, altogether, impressed you strongly with this idea. This person called himself Jacques Roquet. He had fallen in with the Duke's party, as they were returning home, and representing himself as a friar belonging to a small, half-starved order, whose abode was some distance off, had begged that he might be allowed to take advantage of the safe escort, the Duke's train afforded him. By thus representing himself he had received permission to follow in the train of the Duke, by which means he gained admission to the castle, where he was now seated at the board, as we have already said, and watched with a careful eye every thing that was passing around him.

The voice of mirth now broke forth from the revellers in frequent and wild bursts of laughter, plainly declaring, that the "spirit of the vine," had already begun its work. The Duke after an old man's custom, was recounting to those around him, the manœuvres, stratagems, and other incidents of the fight, in which he had borne a share; the ladies were engaged, some in listening to the recital of a perilous enterprize undertaken by some bold knight, others in listening to the words of gallants trained in courts and versed in the arts of love; when suddenly an alarm was heard from the battlements, and in a few moments after, the clashing of weapons, and angry voices of men, as if within the court-yard. And now for the first time it was observed that Roquet was missing, which at once gave rise to suspicions that he was the secret emissary of some enemy, who having assumed the character of a friar, in order that he might gain admission into the castle, had now betrayed it into the hands of the enemy. These suspicions had scarcely arisen, and the astonishment consequent upon the sounds that arose from the court-yard, had not yet given place to any movement or enquiry on the part of the revellers (for they stood looking upon each other as if lost in wonder and uncertainty,) when the door was burst open and

w*

several armed men rushed into the hall. Now commenced a scene of horror and tumult. The revellers sprung up from their seats, and laying their hands upon whatever weapons they could find, began a determined and stout resistance; Charles Moray seized Ellen, and followed by the young lord Foscales, and one or two more, who bore off the other ladies, retreated through the opposite door of the hall, by which he was enabled to gain the eastern part of the castle, in which he knew there would be safety, at least for a time, from any violence. As soon as the ladies were borne to this place of safety, Moray and the other knights returned to the hall, where they beheld a scene of terrible confusion and slaughter—weapons brandishing and clashing in all directions, men fighting pell-mell, some who had been enemies—bitter enemies for years, closed in a deadly embrace; others, who were slain strewed over the floor, and among these lord Henry of Lorraine himself. At the sight of this scene of horror and slaughter, Moray forgetting all considerations of his own safety, followed by the other knights, rushed into the thickest of the fight, and bearing down all that came within their reach, for a moment checked the fury of the assailants.— But this was now of no avail. The most of the Duke's party lay stretched upon the floor.— This Moray saw, and deeming resistance under such circumstances, at best but an act of desperation, he resolved to make good his retreat, hoping at least that he would be able to bear off Ellen in safety from the castle. Having formed this determination, he fought his way to a door, through which he made good his retreat from the hall, which was soon filled alone, by the assailants, the wounded, and the dead.

The ladies who had been conveyed by Moray and the other knights, to the eastern part of the building had all made their escape except Ellen, who anxious for the safety of her father and lover, determined to await the issue of the affair, where she was, believing that, at all events, no matter how ruthless and barbarous the assailants might be, her sex would serve her as a protection against all outrage. She had not however been long alone, before she heard the silent and cautious tread of some one approaching the part of the building where she was. These steps now grew nearer, and presently she heard a low voice asking admission, which she immediately recognized as Moray's. She now unbolted the door, when her lover stood before her pale and sprinkled with blood, as the moon-beams, that now shone through a window of the castle, enabled her to perceive. At the sight of Moray thus pale and bloody, she was about to scream out, when grasping her by the hand he entreated her in the name of heaven, not to utter a word, but silently and cautiously follow him.

"What?" demanded Ellen, "leave the castle, and my father still in it? No, Moray, I shall not stir from this spot, as long as any one I hold dear remains in it. But why has not my father been here for me?—he surely has not been slain;" and her breath grew quick as she asked the question.

"It would be vain Ellen," replied Moray, "for me to conceal the fact. Lord Henry lies low among the dead. He fell by the hand of his most inveterate enemy."

Ellen now wrung her hands in agony as Moray confirmed her fearful suspicions. She stood for some time the picture of mute wretchedness and despair, during which Moray was uncertain whether to bear her off in his arms from this place of danger, or to await with her the approach of the rude soldiery. When recovering from her paroxysm of feeling, and regaining in some degree her usual firmness, she cried—

"And am I then fatherless? A dark foreboding came over me but yesterday, as I sat gazing from the castle window over the plain, expecting the coming of my father, that some calamity would befall me. A terrible one has come, for I am left without kindred in this wide world, and almost without a friend." And as she spoke the tears rolled down her melancholy face.

"Never without a friend and protector," Moray replied with animation, "as long as the God of strength nerves this arm, it shall serve you, though all the dangers of life should beset your path."

"Then," replied Ellen, her spirits reviving, "since every thing, that was dear to me here, has been taken away from me, I am free to follow you, Moray, wherever you may lead the way. But would it not be better to remain here," she observed, as she thought upon the dangers that would attend their flight, "and trust rather to the gene-

rosity of the enemy, than encounter the dangers
that will attend upon an attempt to escape."

"No! never," replied Moray, "you know not Ellen, in whose power you would throw yourself.—
Let us haste speedily hence, I pray you, for a short
delay may place you in the hands of lord Robert
of Fontenaye."

"Of whom?" demanded Ellen, "of Robert of
Fontenaye!—the dark and deadly sir Robert!"

"Yes, Robert of Fontenaye," replied Moray,
"the ancient and inveterate enemy of your house,
is the leader of this attack upon the castle, and
were he to find you here, there is no telling what
deeds his dark and hellish spirit would prompt him
to. He would leave no means untried to make
you his victim."

"He certainly would not use force against a woman," replied Ellen. "The vilest miscreant on
earth, would scarcely do an act so cowardly, as to
offer injury to the weak."

"Trust not Ellen," Moray replied, "to such an
one as Sir Robert, though he be a noble, and a belt-
ed knight, and one who ought therefore to protect
the sex, yet there is nothing too vile for his doing,

no means so dishonorable, that he will not resort to."

"He is reputed brave in war," answered Ellen, "and though the enemy of my father's house, its implacable enemy, yet he surely would not do aught that would taint the honor of knighthood."

"That he is reputed brave in war," replied Moray, "I will admit; but that any considerations of honor, would deter him from his designs I do not believe. Lord Robert is one who wears a fair face to the world, yet that seeming fairness is but the mask under which he conceals the boldest crimes."

"But whither will you go," demanded Ellen, "after we shall have escaped from the castle.—The surrounding passes will all be guarded by Lord Robert's forces, and we shall thus be prevented, at last, from effecting our escape. Had we not therefore better await where we are the issue of this night's horrors."

"No," replied Moray eagerly, and mingled firmness and high pride, were visibly depicted in his face as he spoke, "I would rather encounter with you all the dangers that we may be liable to at

the hands of a rude soldiery, than that you shoul
remain a moment longer in this castle. Let us
haste hence, I pray you Ellen, for the wolf's den is
no place for the lamb."

Ellen now consented, and Moray leading the
way, they left the room treading with slow and
cautious steps, the winding passages, and rooms,
through which they had to pass to gain the outlet,
by means of which Moray hoped to escape. They
had succeeded in gaining this outlet, and were now
near the edge of the copsewood, which was at the
distance of some two or three hundred yards from
the castle, when they discovered they were pursued by horsemen. They now gained the wood,
from which Moray looking back, thought he recognized the arms and bearing of Robert of Fontenaye, as the light was reflected upon the horsemen
by the pale beams of the now setting moon.—
Knowing that lord Robert could follow with no
other motive than that of recovering Ellen, the
anxious Moray seized the terrified girl in his arms,
and plunging with her into the thickest of the
wood, soon found a place which would afford security to them until the horsemen should pass by.

They remained in this place of concealment for some time, when the pursuers, giving up all hopes of finding those they were in search of, returned to the castle. Moray and Ellen now came forth, and pursuing their way towards the sea coast, found themselves early in the morning, just as the sun was about to burst in all its majesty upon the broad waters before them, near a peasant's cottage in which they sought and received shelter and food. And here we will leave our fugitives, in the enjoyment of the security of the peasant's abode, whilst we carry our reader to other scenes.

It will now be necessary in order to the full developement of our story, that we give a short account of the character and schemes of a powerful noble, and rival of Lord Henry of Lorraine, the baron Robert of Fontenaye.

Robert of Fontenaye was a man of an arbitrary and tyrannic temper—haughty and proud by nature, and without any of that cultivation which, in those days, was possessed by those, who, from their rank or wealth, had it in their power to frequent the courts of the surrounding monarchs, he kept himself aloof from those around him, and thus rendered

x

himself an object rather of notice, than respect.—
These traits of his character displayed themselves
towards his inferiors—his retainers and those over
whom he had power. He was also a man of an
ambitious spirit, and therefore he engaged in all
those wars, that so frequently broke out around
him, not for the love of a soldier's life, as was the
case with the lord of Lorraine, but always with
the latent design of extending his territories, his
wealth and consequently his power and importance.

The Duke of Lorraine had ever stood in his
path, a noble equally powerful with himself, and
of an active and enterprizing spirit, he could not
but be an object of hatred to such an one as Robert
of Fontenaye. For this reason they were ever at
war with each other upon the least pretext that
was afforded. Baron Robert was a dark, designing, intriguing, wily man, who cared not by what
means he secured the accomplishment of his objects, the exact reverse of Lord Henry—who was
bold, frank and undisguised, in all his actions,
from which traits he was the more liable to be en-
snared by the cunning and the wiles of his rival.—

Indeed it often happened that in their frequent feuds, Lord Henry was surprised and led into ambuscades, from which he was only released by the superior prowess and boldness of his soldiery.—Baron Robert in addition to his other characteristicks, was one of those men who seeks your presence always from some hidden motive of advantage. He was cordial in his manner to all those from whom he had any objects to gain. There was always, when in the company of others, a smile upon his face, under which, however, an accurate observer would frequently perceive a lurking expression of bitterness.

His dominions were large and populous, and to render them more so, he encouraged emigration from the surrounding countries into his own; consequently he always had a great many adventurers around him—those, who exiled from their own countries for their crimes, were always willing to enlist under the banners of one, whose ambitious spirit was sure to give them employment and probably distinction.

Among the followers of baron Robert, there was a certain Caspard Cellini, an Italian by birth, who

had been compelled to leave his own country to
escape the punishment that would have overtaken
him, at last, for his many crimes. This Caspard
Cellini was a cunning wily villian, who, like his
master, cared not what atrocities he committed—
what baseness he resorted to, in effecting the execution of his designs. Consequently he was such
an one, as would be useful to baron Róbert in his
plans.

For some years past Robert of Fontenaye had
ceased to molest the Duke. But this seeming quiet
was the quiet of the tiger, who only remains in his
hiding place, in order, the more effectually, to seize
upon his prey. Hearing about this time that there
was to be a great festival at the Duke's castle, baron Robert determined to make use of so fine an
opportunity to accomplish the destruction of his rival. To this end it was planned, that Cellini
should assume the disguise of a friar, and thus attempt to gain admission to the castle, during this
occasion of revelry: by this means he would be
able to open its gates to baron Robert, who would
conceal himself with his forces in the day time, in
the surrounding mountains, and descend into the

plain at night. This design being formed, Cellini set off upon his work of treachery, and falling in with the Duke's train, as they were returning home, had betrayed the castle as is already known to the reader.

*   *   *   *   *   *

It was now some months after the attack upon the castle, and the slaughter and dispersion of its inmates, that Charles Moray and Ellen embarked on board a vessel bound for England. They had concealed themselves in the cottages of the peasantry along the coast, until giving up all hopes of ever regaining possession of the territory of Lorraine, which would now be Moray's in right of Ellen, (his bride) who was the only child of lord Henry, and a vessel bound for England having come upon the coast, in order to lay in a provision of water, Moray determined to embark in it, in hopes that he would find fortune more favorable to him in his own country, than he had done since he left it. And now we find him once more thrown upon the world, after a period of years spent in activity, toil, and hardships, during which time he had risen to a station which the most fortunate

x*

would have deemed an enviable one. He however, consoled himself under the reflection, that he had secured one thing of value, at least, from the wreck of his fortunes in the love of Ellen, and with that buoyant, persevering and active spirit, which adversity could not destroy, he looked forward still to years of distinction and pleasure.

During Moray's absence, one of those revolutions which were at that time so frequent in England had taken place, and the party by whose downfall Moray's father had been exiled, and his family ruined, had now gained the ascendant. All those, who, under the late ruling party, had enjoyed the honors and wealth of the country, were in their turn deprived of their estates, which once more came into the hands of the former owners, at least of that portion of them, whom the violence of the times had left alive to claim them. Moray upon his landing hearing of this change that had take place in his absence, and seeing in it the revival of all the former honors of his house, resolved to repair immediately to his Monarch, and solicit from him the restoration of his family estates. He did so, and his request was granted, not only on account of his being the only descendant of a long, powerful family, but also for his prowess upon the continent, the fame of which had found its way even into his own country. Moray now soon arose to great influence in his own country, and became distinguished both as a soldier and a statesman— great alike in the camp and court. And here at this fortunate period of his life, happy in the enjoyment of all those delights which attend upon a life of great and good actions, rich too, in the possession of a lovely wife, whose beauties were only surpassed by her virtues, we will take leave of Charles Moray the exiled adventurer.

LINES.

I saw a cloud upon the eastern sky
'Twas glowing in the crimson of the morn,
And burnish'd by the glorious golden sun;
It faded, pass'd and with the ether mingled.
Thus infant beauty glows in life's young morn
In sickness fades, evaporates and joins
The sublimated atmosphere of Heaven.

TO ——

You ask me why, when nature throws
    Her charms around, my soul is sad,
And why dark gloom is on my brow,
    When every youthful heart is glad?

I strike the lyre but 'tis in vain,
    It will not breathe one note of gladness;
And when I smile at other's joys,
    It but unveils my bosom's sadness.

When the fond mother o'er her boy
    Is bending with an anguish'd heart,
Whose pallid cheek and glassy eye
    Too plainly tell that they must part,

Oh! will not tones of joy and mirth,
    Fall harshly on that mother's ear,
While weeping o'er the couch of one
    Who soon will press the fun'ral bier?

Then ask me not to smile again
  Or breathe to thee one note of gladness,
It would but give thy bosom pain
  To know my heart is filled with sadness.

                            E.

SONNET.

How fragrant is the breath
Of the young vernal morn!
How sweet the crimson dye
That evening clouds adorn!

More fragrant are the sighs
That strong affection prove,
More sweet the modest blush
That dyes the cheek of love!

And softer than the gleam
Of Hesper in the sky,
Is the gently thrilling beam
Of love's soft lustrous eye!

JULIA NELSON.

BY MARIA WILLIAMS.

He tore the rose-bud from the parent stalk,
And trampling on it, left it to the storm.

WHITE.

"MEET me at the fountain, as the moon is setting and beyond the reach of thy cruel father, the winds shall waft us to a clime, where blessed with each other's love, months and years of superlative bliss shall roll around."

Thus spoke a young Venetian to a beautiful English maiden of sixteen, whose affections he had won, and who continued to receive his visits clandestinely, after he had been forbidden her father's house—Julia consented. The clock struck four. The beams of the declining moon were silvering the dusky battlements of her father's Chateau and the towering elms that encircled it. She quitted her apartment and muffling up her face in her cloak hastened to the appointed place. She gazed in tearful agony on the home she was leaving forever —and throwing her arms around Tremoni's neck, wept aloud. When this burst of feeling was over, "lead on" said she, "I go whithersoever thou wilt," and being handed into the boat she was soon at the ship, which was to convey her to Venice.

The morning rose bright and beautiful upon the earth and the gallant ship expanding her snowy pinions to the breeze, skimmed along the surface of the sea like an inhabitant of air.

The eyes of Julia were turned to the receding beach. There stood her agonized father and there waved the hand of her frantic mother. Her eyes were suffused with moisture as she looked, and the melting sympathies of nature bedewed her cheeks; but the countenance of Tremoni beaming with glowing affection, softened by pity, mitigated her sorrow and she gazed in mute and subdued woe upon her parents, till they lessened, became a speck, and vanished from the sight.

In Venice they were married and Julia was happy so long as the novelty of her society delighted the libertine Tremoni. Indifference, unkindness and cold neglect followed, and Julia wept for the sympathies of parental affection which she had abandoned for the false love of a heartless libertine. A splendid city establishment, together with a country residence on the Brenta, a magnificent equipage, with vast sums expended on the abandoned and at the gaming table soon exhausted the wealth of Tremoni and he longed for the death of his innocent spouse, that by an union with the infamous Madame A—— of immense estate, he might repair his fallen fortunes

* * * * * * * *

It was a dark and stormy night. The wind swept awfully o'er the plain, the agitated billows of the Brenta roared and dashed heavily against the craggy shore, the fitful lightning streamed along the darkened sky, and the rumbling thunder pealed from the blazing heaven. Tremoni passing around the point of a promontory with Julia, stood at the mouth of a horrid cavern. He urged her forward, while her shrieks reverberated along the hollow recesses.— At a distance far within a glimmering torch threw around its pale rays. He drew her towards the light, when horrrible! there yawned at her feet a newly-dug grave. She implored life by every expression, which fear or the love of existence could suggest; but the monster's heart was steeled against pity and seizing her long tresses by one hand, he drew her over the grave, and with the other aimed the fatal poniard, when the lightning fell tremendous over their heads and bursting through the rocky ceiling, glared in awful brilliance around.—Tremoni hesitated, his eyes evinced terror. "Desist Tremoni," said Julia, "the wrath of Heaven will avenge my death." But again the poniard was drawn and aimed at the breast of the shrieking Julia, when the lightning directed by the arm of Omnipotence descended upon the murderer's head and struck him lifeless into the grave he had dug for his innocent wife.

Julia with an only daughter, sought her country and kindred, and in the affection of a forgiving father and the tenderness of a soothing mother, in a measure regained the happiness, which had smiled upon her youth.

Y

RENOVATION.

BY LUCIUS D'ALMONDI.

'Tis night,
The darken'd clouds their dusky mantles spread,
In gloom extended, o'er the rayless sky,
Save where the gleam of Phosphor, pledge of day,
Faint twinkles through the curtains of the east.
The darken'd clouds now soften into gray,
Now heighten into purple and bright gold.
More faintly twinkles Phosphor's feeble ray,
While, as it fades and vanishes from sight,
Obscur'd by beams of fulgence far transcendent,
Lo! the Sun, bursting in glory on the darksome
     earth
Pours the bright day o'er verdant isle and sea.
               'Tis morn.
Like waving canvass, on the sky, the clouds
Painted in hues of glory richly glow,
The mountain-tops with light are blazing, and the
     streams

Like liquid silver flash beneath its ray,
The Earth with robe of varied dyes adorn'd
Looks bright and beautiful.　All nature smiles
In renovated light and life and joy.

So when the sun of life has set to man,
Thick clouds of darkness gather round the tomb.
Hope's cheering star through dusky shadows gleam
The promise of a resurrection morn.
At length, the breaking clouds shall melt away
Before the coming of the genial light.
Hope's waning star is lost amid the blaze
Of that eternal Sun, that pours the beams
Of endless morning.——Heav'ns effulgent rays
Empyrean brightness shed on all around,
And wake to light, life and eternal joy
The sleeping spirits of the mouldering dead.

THE THUNDER STORM.

BY T. I. LEAKIN.

Cœlo tonantem credidimus Jovem regnare.—HORATIUS.

THERE is a hardness in the human breast, which few external circumstances can act on. We see pain and disease, the precursors of death, devastating our friends, and yet consider not our "latter end." We daily behold our fellow-mortals like leaves in autumn falling around us. The hearse in all the pomp and grandeur of majestic woe, with its plumes vibrating to the wind and the long train of sable habiliments, affect us no more than the "sounding brass or the tinkling cymbal." Perhaps some sensitive soul may for a moment give a passing sigh as the corpse is carried along to its narrow tenement—but, then—'tis evanescent—fleeting as the shadow which passeth away, and abideth not. Indeed it would seem that the heart of man is formed of impenetrable materials—nought can make him stand aghast, paralize his soul, and

literally shrink him into his own insignificance,—
save the red right arm of Heaven,—the scathing
lightning, or the withering, blasting thunderbolt of
HIM, who "rides in the whirlwind and propels
the storm." The Atheist may, in moments of nature's quiet, wrap and wind himself close in the
folds of his garment of non-existence beyond the
grave;—the Deist also, indulge in those intervals
of calm placidity, (and too often illusive serenity)
in his favorite visionary sophism,—"as the tree
falleth, so it lies"—yet should the "GREAT GOD"
illuminate and set the Heaven's in a blaze with the
awful and tremendous corruscations of his wrath,
and rock our little ball with the thunders of his
displeasure—'tis *then*, the ungodly, blustering, bully-
ing bravado is suddenly transformed into the trembling coward, his limbs become palsied, and his knees
smite together like those of Belteshazzar—and
could we but have a survey of the inward workings of his soul, there would be discovered, inscribed in plain and legible characters—THERE IS A
GOD.

Y*

PITY.

BY EMILIA PURNELL.

The petals of a modest flower
   Expanded to my view,
Its beauteous cups, fill'd with a shower,
   Of pure and heavenly dew.

When grief and care and snares arise,
   And the faint soul beset,
Thus have I seen soft Pity's eyes
   With heavenly moisture wet.

As o'er the air-harp's silken cords
   The placid zephyrs stole,
Music more soft than singing birds,
   Shed sweetness o'er my soul.

And thus, when sorrow's sighs and moans
   Her soul's fine chords have stirr'd,
Sweet as the air-harp's silver tones
   Soft Pity's voice is heard.

The lonely star of eve did gleam,
  As light from earth was fled,
And shed a soft and gentle beam
  Above my darken'd head.

And thus soft Pity's eye will shed
  A light upon the soul,
When every ray of Joy is fled,
  And clouds of darkness roll.

ROMANCE.

'NEATH the shade of sylvan bower,
By the side of ruin'd tower,
By the legendary cell,
By the sparkling fairy well,
Where the leaping cascades pour
Down the cliff with heavy roar,
Where the obelisk displays
Trophies won in ancient days,
Where the glimm'ring pale moonbeam
Dances on the trembling stream,
Lost in musing's dewy pow'r,
Romance loves to while the hour.

THE SCEPTIC'S SOLILOQUY.

I STAND amidst the dissolving ruins of wrecked creation, the sun is blown out, the moon is turned to blood, the firmament is rolling away like a scroll, systems are broken up, planets are flying to and fro through this void immense—Nature in convulsions is heaving forth her expiring groans. Time, space and matter as though frightened at the uproar of the conflict, seem fleeing for shelter from this scene of destruction, and the last gleam of light is now breaking upon this universal chaos of night and ruin.

Ye stars! which anon in heaven's blue concave hung pendent out as the jewelry of night, sending forth your twinkling beams to irradiate and beautify the shades of darkness, now I behold you not as then smiling in beauty, and, from afar trembling forth your tiny rays of light, as you moved in the most majestic grandeur through unbounded space,

but shorn of your beauty, and deserted by your loveliness, you now appear as so many fearful harbin-
gers of woe and destruction.

But how is this.   Death and ruin are either an-
nihilating or destroying every thing around: ani-
mate and inanimate existences, are alike passing
from being, yet here am I untouched.   The clouds of
destruction—big with ruin and black with the com-
bustibles of death, though hovering around yet
leave me unharmed; of all creation I, man alone,
am permitted to view this scene as if superior to it,
    alone can contemplate unmoved the annihilation
of the last fragment of matter.   Can it be, that I
really am superior to these things, or is it in truth
only some idle thought, some phantasm of the
brain, which suggests these notions.   Man is mortal,—for what else can he be.   Avaunt misgiv-
ings! for even in this dread hour of danger and
dismay, I will not be frightened into the belief of an
Hereafter, and an eternity of existence.   It cannot,
cannot be.   The everlasting hills, though clothed
in eternal verdure; the gigantic mountains, though
piled up till their brows look down upon the regions
of the clouds; the mighty rivers, though winding

through and fertilizing the sequestered spots of earth; the great ocean, from whose vast depths are sent forth the clouds of rain; nay, this earth, and the system of which it is a part, all, bear marks of final and inevitable dissolution—for it is stamped, as reason informs her enlightened followers, upon every thing of creation. And shall man, vain man, feed himself with the notion that he is superior to all these things, and that after all other exist-ences have long since passed away, the immortal principle which some fancy he has within him, shall flourish in eternal youth, vigor and felicity in some far distant and happy clime? Childish, un-reasonable thought—the offspring of pride and the bantling of vanity. The carcase of the most pow-erful animal, soon becomes the prey of the vulture, fertile fields become barren; the magnificent palace a ruin; the populous city a desert; the sturdy and far spreading oak, whose beautiful foliage has been fanned by the winds of a thousand summers, after ages of decay at last crumbles into dust; and man, proud man, in turn must die, and as his body is commingling with the dust of the valley, wild ani-mals browse upon his unhonored grave. But what am I when produced and for what end? I am—I can be nothing else than mere matter, and if annihilation is the certain end of all material things, then is my history known. But calculations about this stupendous scene before me never entered into the schemes of my philosophy. And yet it cannot be that I was wrong, seeing that reason guided me in every thing, but here is an occurrence that was not considered even as contingent, its existence augurs some thing erroneous. Let me try again, what reason says upon the subject; she cannot teach me wrong, and to her decisions I will bow with reverence. Well then, I cannot believe that things exist by chance, for reason no more informs me so than it does the contrary—no, nor not as much, for as every thing produced must, in a greater or less degree, bear the impress of the source from whence it proceeds, regularity cannot proceed from chance —nor certainty be the offspring of uncertainty. More—could chance after having produced innumerable worlds, with all their attendant satellites and belts, and arranged them into systems, with their suns and comets, have ordained each sun with his retinue of worlds, besides their daily and annual

revolutions to perform immense circles through
illimitable space around some great and universal
centre: could mere chance have done this? No!—
Certainly not—for this as well as every thing else,
in being's endless chain, from the insignificant Zoo-
phytes to the Leviathan whose huge bulk floats securely in the northern seas; or the fearful polypi,
which slumber securely in the recesses of the un-
fathomed profound of the ocean; from the insect
that has but a microscopic existence, to the fearless
lion which scours the pathless desert in search of
danger, or the soaring eagle which utters his wild
scream of superiority in the higher regions of the
air; from a pebble to the whole grand orrery of
creation, where worlds convoying worlds, float
on in their apparently eternal courses.—All, all, as
a continued argument go to prove, that they are,
and exist in the most perfect order and regularity:
and that their creation as well as existence demon-
strates a design. But what is this inscrutable design? What object could the beings who were
wise and powerful enough to create a world, have
had in view when this was produced? Was it done
from whim or caprice?—all wise beings are inca-

pable of folly. Was it done to display their power?—that cannot be, for none but their own creatures could ever have come to any knowledge of it.
Such motives as these and the like could never have
operated upon all wise and good beings. For what
then, was this world created? 'Tis said by some that
it was originally called into being by a supreme
power, who entered into it as its soul or essence,
and that the things thereof were created for one-
another respectively, that every thing has an inde-
pendent, relative existence. But if this was the
case, would we not find an universal equality on
earth? Would not every thing be reduced to a
common level? No such state as this ever did
exist. Now, as where there is no equality, superiority must be somewhere, let us consider if the
world was made for man or man for the world.—
Did the infinite beings, who were the authors of all
creation, in the superabundance of their wisdom,
and plenitude of their power, call man into existence
merely to admire the beautiful structure of the globe,
to climb the mountains, to sail the ocean, to till the
earth, to gaze at the sun, to wonder at the stars, to
be amazed at the comets, and, finally to die; for the

z

purpose of giving death a victim, sinking to nothing and forgetfulness, without even oblivion's wing flapping, above that mouldering body, where, once, as some say, a proud spirit dwelt, and where now it may be the slimy worms of earth hold revels and banquetings—natural reason indignantly regrets so degrading a view of the subject, and to its dictates I bow; for it declares, that nature and nature's God alike proclaim, that the earth was made for man; that the caverns in the bowels of the mountain are filled with water for the purpose of fertilizing the earth, and making it conduce to the comfort of man; that the lightnings which leap with vivid brightness athwart the heavens, accompanied at times with such tremendous peals of thunder as to make nature herself seem to tremble with affright, by cleansing and purifying the atmosphere are made to subserve the purposes of man's health; the furious storms by scattering miasma and effluvia go to insure the same end; the great deep, the waters of which are spread out by every land, and whose exhalations by refreshing and moistening the air, and sustaining vegetation, are made to perform its part in this grand scheme of man's support.—

And also, the thousand arms of the ocean as they meander through the silent groves, the fertile vallies, the cultivated fields, the orchards, vineyards, and gardens of man, by facilitating the interchange of both the necessaries and luxuries of life, tend to promote the happiness of man; nay, the motion of the earth itself, gives him the agreeable change of seasons and of the hours of labour and rest; these and many other things all go to prove that the earth was made for man. But what wild chain of bewildered thought am I pursuing? What labyrinth of religious folly and bigotry am I entering? man is not, he cannot be, superior to the brutes— and, yet—oh strange and wayward disposition of man! I am now half inclined to believe the contrary—reason, can teach me nothing but what is right; my belief is therefore fixed in what she says. So let me follow out a little farther these thoughts:— Now, if there is nothing without design in all of nature's works; what was the design of making man lord of the creation, and enduing him with a mind, was it merely that he might have a superiority of being over his fellow creatures? No, for a common end would in a great measure have des-

troyed this distinction, and nature does nothing in
vain, if man is really lord of creation and endowed
with all the powers and attributes of mind, then
must I believe in despite of my former doubts, that
he has a superiority of existence over the rest of
creation, that his nature is more elevated, the purposes and end of his being transcendently noble
over every thing of earth; reason declares—and, I
must believe these things—but is there such a thing
as this mind, does that subtle principle which is
within us and which I am conscious at this moment thinks in reality, constitute a different part of
my existence, distinct and separate from my material body; is it an immaterial essence originally
pure, and holy, which was breathed into my cor-
rupt and sinful body at the dawn of creation, while
yet the first fruits thereof, were chanting anthems
of praise to that power which had spoken a world
from nought?—or is it—as many have taught, and
I sometimes believed only the effects of my particular organization, the natural result of the form
and combination of the different parts of my body;
a material, palpable something, whose existence
must consequently be short and evanescent, as its

origin is base and ignoble? I cannot now believe this, for if the mind be nothing but the effect of the union of the different parts of the body, then would we find them always conjoined, but natural idiots though capable of performing most bodily functions are nevertheless entirely devoid of mind, then I think, that as the mind thus exists it is an immaterial, and separate part of man; and if so, it must be superior to mere matter, for its immaterial qualities cannot be affected by the convulsions, on even extinction, of the material world, it must then belong to a superior and far more elevated order of existences; but where is this superiority to be enjoyed, is it only before our fellow worms that this excellence is to be shewn forth, and was this world of toil indeed originally intended as a place of rest, and are mankind destined as some philosophers have taught to go on increasing and progressing in knowledge and information, until in the fullness of their wisdom, they shall succeed in exterminating from earth, every species of vice and sickness; when death and all other evils being entirely banished, man shall be allowed to live in a continued round of peace, happiness and prospe-

z*

rity? Alas! no, the very perfection of the picture is a sufficient contradiction of its truth, the too faithful history of man informs us, that in time gone by, what one age has done the next has undone, what one generation has learned another has forgotten; that the mind of man has always thus vacillated between a high degree of knowledge and absolute ignorance. Can reason then assent to the proposition that this world is the allotted place for man to enjoy the felicity, which his extraordinary powers, shew he was destined for. No, surely not; for neither nature, nor nature's God, can be at fault in their arrangement, which would be the case if this was destined as a place of bliss; for daily experience proves to us, that in life man is as pre-eminent in misery as happiness; if these things are so, man cannot die and cease to be, if he is thus, there must be an hereafter and an eternity of existence, and the thick shades which now overhang futurity, must, when pierced, reveal to us an other and a different state of being. The curtain, which the convulsions of death rend, must display to the disenthralled soul, some blissful region, where our immortal powers can dilate in the enjoyment of supreme and eternal felicity; for the bounds of this little world, the surface of this atom of creation are by far too small for the longings and aspirations of such a being as reason proves man to be. Now if reason will go thus far, it must go farther, and allow if man is thus he must originally have been made so, by the first great cause of existence, and also, that this cause must be far superior to what man its creature is. The fabric of the universe speaks forth its powers; for though creation is spread before us, our minds are found by far too limited to grasp at a single view the whole of its stupendous parts, and the first cause of all existence must necessarily be uncaused; but if I believe this, will it not be giving up one system of dogmas for another; casting off pantheism merely to put on polytheism? Surely not, for as it required an omnipotent as well as omniscient being to do these things, no such one can have equals, as polytheism would teach—therefore, I am forced to believe that creation must have been the work of one all-wise and powerful God. Now, if I was created by this God, and endowed by him with certain powers and principles which cannot be enjoyed here, would he be acting the part of such a being to let me live in ignorance of what means I might best enjoy my powers, and fulfil the end of my existence? No, for to act so would be contrary to his very nature, such a being must necessarily adopt the best means to gain his proposed end, which this would be the very reverse of doing; therefore, not only is there one great God, but as we came into the world ignorant of these things, he must in accordance with his very nature, have revealed them to us. Impossible!!—Can this be a reasonable conclusion, have I been mistaken for a long life in supposing that reason and revelation were two things opposite alike in their nature and tendencies—can the whole of this be sustained by reason? It, is—then must I receive and believe it; but who is this being to whom the adoration of all creation should ascend, this king of immensity, this monarch of eternal duration; who is he that necessarily existing from everlasting to everlasting, can have neither beginning of years nor end of days?—reason, conscience and revelation alike point to thee, *Jehovah*,—thou art he who hast done these things, thou king of kings and lord

of lords—thou and thou only can be, and art the
very God; it is thou who traces the courses of time
and grasps the destinies of eternity. Alas!—alas!—
to think that nothing but the terrific sublimity of a
judgment day could have taught me this.   But now,
I know, where the immortal, though at present im-
prisoned, soul of man shall flourish in eternal felicity, where that never dying particle of divinity
which we have within us, shall bloom with resplendent beauty when time shall have long been forgotten, and eternity shall have progressed in an
immeasurable round of ages; for it shall join the
redeemed of earth in chanting amidst the flowery
fields and balmy groves of heaven, everlasting anthems of praise to the first great cause of existence,
for he hath said that "where I am ye shall be also."

And shall I, man, be for ever linked to that being
—an inhabitant of eternity—an actor in the scenes
of which the lapse of time despairs a distant end.—
And can it be that this life is but the twilight, the
dim dawn of an eternal one, and that instead of being placed here to languish out a few years of pain,
misery and insignificance, to be the sport of fortune,
the toy of delusion, and eternally transported and

alarmed at the petty strifes around us, enjoying a mere existence without either purpose or end, and then dying like the worn-out brute upon the commons, we are destined to have a perpetuity of blissful existence surrounded by happy spirits in an eternal world. And can eternity belong to man? Can a being so frail—so unstable—so insignificant as man, really claim eternity as his? Can it be that the stirrings that we feel within us—that inciting hope—buoyant joy—restless ambition and the like are but scintillations of an eternity of existence; that our discontent of a mere earthly life—and secret and constant yearnings after a different and a better state of being—are nothing but the shadows which a coming futurity casts before us. That life is but a weary pilgrimage which mortality has to perform as a penance for existence, before we are admitted into the world of spirits—and that in truth these bodies are nothing, as it were, but vessels in which our souls are fast sailing upon the great ocean of time to a never ending eternity.— Yes 'tis so—*Conscience*, that secret monitor within us, attests its truth—reason supports and a thousand proofs go to demonstrate it—in doubting it

sceptics ye cheat yourselves and delude your followers—for if there be a happy hereafter, by acting
wise and virtuously we shall certainly obtain it,
and if there is not we cannot loose it.   So that in
either case to gain by following you is impossible—
your creed then must be folly and your disciple-
ship vexation of spirit—and you can only pretend
to disbelieve the system of religion—because your
pride prompts you to reject that which you find
your limited faculties unable to comprehend.   But
what is it you purpose giving us for this pleasing
hope of immortality, this cheering expectation
that when we are done with the sorrows of time we
shall be able to partake of the joys of eternity—for
the consoling reflection, that the troubles of earth
will only give us the greater zest for the pleasures
of heaven—for the consciousness, that when we
shall find ourselves struggling in the last agonies of
death, when time and the things thereof are fast
fading from our failing visions, when with a last
convulsive throe our breath shall be yielded, instead
of sinking into an empty nothingness, a dark vacui-
ty, we shall be able while surveying the vast horizon of immensity,which will then be spread before

us, to hail the twinkling of a far distant beam of light the beacon of eternity—the morning star of glory—by which we shall be guided through the intricacies of the labyrinth of death, to where we shall join the happy multitudes in everlasting felicity in paying unceasing orisons to the great eternal. Can you proffer us nothing in exchange for all this but *the promise* of a cold dreary and comfortless *oblivion.* J. H. C.

THE END.

Check Out More Titles From HardPress Classics Series In this collection we are offering thousands of classic and hard to find books. This series spans a vast array of subjects – so you are bound to find something of interest to enjoy reading and learning about.

Subjects:
Architecture
Art
Biography & Autobiography
Body, Mind &Spirit
Children & Young Adult
Dramas
Education
Fiction
History
Language Arts & Disciplines
Law
Literary Collections
Music
Poetry
Psychology
Science
…and many more.

Visit us at www.hardpress.net

CPSIA information can be obtained
at www.ICGtesting.com
Printed in the USA
BVHW091904220819
556561BV00021B/4818/P